Jesus said, "A new comma1
In this exuberant, funny, a1
sign allows us not just to serve, but actually to love, people we will never meet. It is common for economists to praise the utility of the market, but Carden explains the moral necessity of a presumption in favor of liberty well-used in the service of God.

—Mike Munger, Duke University

You're a Christian. Good. But you think the economy is contrary to Christianity. Not good. Professor Carden sets you straight, painlessly. Read it, then go and sin no more.

—Deirdre N. McCloskey

If an agnostic Jew like me could enjoy this enlightening series of essays by Christian and economist Art Carden, surely many others can. In *Strangers with Candy*, the learned Dr. Carden shares his learning with a light touch--and he invites us all to delight in it.

—Gene Epstein, Soho Forum Director and former Economics Editor at Barron's Financial Weekly.

*Strangers with Candy* is an excellent approach to the economic way of thinking in which we learn about how the basic principles of economics are a powerful framework to both understand and improve the world. This accessible and enjoyable book is a story of the catallactic process of the market, widening the circles of exchange through the market and transforming strangers into trustworthy and yet anonymous members of the community. Trade is made of win and yes, you can and should trust strangers in the marketplace.

—Anne Bradley, Vice President of Academic Affairs, The Fund for American Studies

*Strangers with Candy* explores the unintended consequences of our economic choices and actions. It shows how economics can help us better understand when we should and shouldn't worry, and how we can best help others. A must-read for anyone interested in the intersection of economics and Christian faith.

—Bard AI (because we couldn't resist asking!)

As a pastor of a church in a global city, I want to help my people understand how the gospel applies to every area of life: family, work, how we shop, and where we live. Dr. Carden attests that 'economics is everywhere' and does so from a unique perspective as a Christian applying the gospel to his work. *Strangers with Candy* is a fantastic book which attempts to show how thoughtful economics can be a means to love one's neighbor and bless others through discovering how to use one's resources for the good of others and the advancement of the Kingdom of God. By challenging common misconceptions and well-intentioned axioms, Dr. Carden gives a path forward for those looking to think seriously about how money is a means to be a blessing.

—Steven Castello, Lead Pastor, City on a Hill Church: Forest Hills, Boston, MA

Art Carden's love—for the discipline of economics, yes, but also his family, his students, and his calling—shines through in *Strangers with Candy*, preparing readers to love *our* neighbors more effectively. No matter one's existing level of economic literacy, I trust this book will leave you, as it did me, with a fresh view on the big, enduring questions that matter for human flourishing and appreciating its plethora of concrete examples, Art's careful articulation, and his invitational, approachable writing style.

—Sarah M. Estelle, Professor of Economics, Hope College and econisforlovers.com

# STRANGERS WITH CANDY

## OBSERVATIONS FROM THE ORDINARY BUSINESS OF LIFE

**ART CARDEN**

*Strangers with Candy: Observations from the Ordinary Business of Life*

© Copyright 2023 The Libertarian Christian Institute. All rights reserved. except for brief quotations in critical publications or reviews, no part of this book may be reproduced in any manner without prior written permission from the publisher.

Libertarian Christian Institute Press
www.libertarianchristians.com

ISBN: 978-1-7336584-5-4

Except where noted otherwise, Scripture quotations are from New Revised Standard Version Bible, copyright © 1989 National Council of the Churches of Christ in the United States of America. Used by permission. All rights reserved worldwide.

*To my 7th Grade English teacher Mrs. McCray, to whom I promised a dedication for my first book and am sort of making good on that since this is my first solo authored book.*

*And for Shannon, Jacob, Taylor Grace, and David: most of the good we do in the world will be for people we will never meet.*

# CONTENTS

Acknowledgments ..................................................................................I

Foreword ..................................................................................................3

1. Introduction and Plan of the Work: Let's Look Out the Window ............5

## PART I: THINGS HAVE NEVER BEEN BETTER, AND THERE'S NO LIMIT ON THE HORIZON

2. The Past is a Nice Place to Visit. You Wouldn't Want to Live There........11
3. Markets Aren't Magic, But They Are Marvelous ...........................................19
4. The Self-Interest of Strangers Can Lead to a Symphony of Creation ......................................................................................................................25
5. A Mundane Miracle: Recorded Music.............................................................31
6. Turn That Racket Down! Music and Economic Progress..........................37
7. Slinging Webs in the Unlimited Creative Spider-Verse ............................41
8. Ho-Hum. Guess I'll Play Chess With A Stranger on the Other Side of the World........................................................................................................45

## PART II: LENDING STRANGERS A HELPING (INVISIBLE) HAND

9. How to Talk to Strangers: Adam Smith and the Invisible Hand..............53
10. Beer or Grape-Nuts? ...........................................................................................65

11. You Want *How Much* for an Undershirt? ..................................................69
12. How Do You Get to the Studio? Ask a Stranger ...................................73
13. Innovate to Help Strangers During Pandemics ....................................77
14. How Much For that Doggy at the Sushi Bar? .......................................83
15. You Need to Pay Your Employees With The Right Combination of Money and Drugs ..................................................................................87
16. The Market Loves You—and Your Little Dog, Too. ..............................91

## PART III: GOOD NAMES AND GREAT RICHES: HOW STRANGERS HELP YOU AVOID GETTING RIPPED OFF

17. Can the Market Protect You From a Bad Haircut? ..............................97
18. Yes, You Can Be Too Careful: There is Such Thing as Too Much Safety ........................................................................................................101
19. Strangers Help You Avoid Getting Ripped Off ...................................105
20. Planning and the Pokemon Problem ...................................................109
21. Why Can You Trust Strangers With Candy? ........................................113

## PART IV: HOW *NOT* TO HELP STRANGERS

22. Drop Your Phone ....................................................................................119
23. Be a Socialist ...........................................................................................123
24. Be a Communist .....................................................................................129
25. Spend a Ton of Money on "Black Friday" ...........................................133
26. Refuse to Use Self-Checkout To Save Jobs ........................................137
27. Advocate Higher Taxes .........................................................................141
28. Boycott Things Made By Strangers You Want to Help .....................145
29. Stop Strangers From Crossing Borders ..............................................149
30. Tax Goods Made By Foreign Strangers ..............................................153
31. Force Strangers To Use Monopolized Schools .................................159
32. Assume A Stranger With a Plan Can Run Other Strangers' Lives: Pandemics and the Great Mind Fallacy ...............................................167

## Contents

**33.** Say "Necessities Are Too Important To Be Left To The Market" During a Crisis .................................................................... 173
**34.** Make It Illegal to Work For Under $15 An Hour .......................... 179
**35.** Believe That Governments Are Magic ........................................ 183
**36.** Debauch the Currency: The Austrian Theory of the Business Cycle, in Brief ............................................................................. 187
**37.** Throttle Housing Construction and Make It Illegal To Pay More Than a Given Price to Rent An Apartment ................................. 193
**38.** Coddle the American Mind ........................................................ 199
**39.** Enslave People ............................................................................. 205
**40.** How Visions Backed With Violence Make Things Worse ......... 211

### PART V: ORDINARY BUSINESS MAKES A DIFFERENCE

**41.** Business is Public Service ............................................................ 217
**42.** Speculators are Unsung Heroes .................................................. 225
**43.** So is Wandering Oaken from the *Frozen* Movies ..................... 229
**44.** Support Your Local Banker ......................................................... 233
**45.** Is Duke Dropout Zion Williamson Wasting His Life? .............. 235
**46.** Bounty Hunters and Privateers: The Lesson of *The Mandalorian* ....... 239
**47.** Free Markets can Still Get the Job Done .................................... 243
**48.** Lobbying: Like Robbing a Record Store ................................... 249
**49.** Think Harder About Smoke on the Water and Fire in the Sky: Externalities .................................................................................. 253
**50.** Coda: Why Economics is Crucial for Ethical Reflection .......... 261

References and Further Reading ........................................................ 269
Endnotes ................................................................................................ 279
Index ...................................................................................................... 283
About the Libertarian Christian Institute ......................................... 291
The Libertarian Christian Institute's Core Values ............................ 293

# STRANGERS WITH CANDY

### OBSERVATIONS FROM THE ORDINARY BUSINESS OF LIFE

# ACKNOWLEDGMENTS

My intellectual debts are too numerous to name. Donald J. Boudreaux, Bryan Caplan, Tyler Cowen, David Friedman, Mike Hammock, David Henderson, Steven Horwitz, Steven Landsburg, Deirdre McCloskey, Joel Mokyr, Michael Munger, John V.C. Nye, Sarah Skwire, and Walter Williams (who I met once) have influenced me. I read Landsburg's *Price Theory and Its Applications* when I took intermediate microeconomics and then taught from it when I taught Rhodes College's weird-ish introductory microeconomics class that included consumer theory. His popular books like *Fair Play* and *The Armchair Economist* continue to challenge me, and I was thrilled to meet him at a conference in 2022. Among people I haven't met, I owe particular debts to Robin Hanson, Tim Harford, and Thomas Sowell. Sowell's *A Conflict of Visions*, which I first read as a first-year assistant professor, changed how I see the world. My usual lunch crowds at Rhodes College and now Samford University have been and continue to be inspiring sources of new ideas. Nita Ghei, Jon Murphy, and Tim Theus read early versions. Sydney Rennich and Tim Theus assisted with preparing it for publication. Grant money from the Charles Koch Foundation paid for research assistance at various stages. I owe parts of this to a collaboration with Deirdre McCloskey that generated a few articles and our 2020 book *Leave Me Alone and I'll Make You Rich: How the Bourgeois*

*Deal Enriched the World* (Chicago: University of Chicago Press). Jeffrey Tucker guided my first wobbly steps into public commentary for the Ludwig von Mises Institute and later at the American Institute for Economic Research, where he was editor when I wrote most of these articles.

Ultimately, the book is for Shannon and the kids—Jacob, Taylor Grace, and David. I write that you may have a better world.

# FOREWORD

Libertarians, economists, and especially libertarian economists get a bad rap. In the popular imagination, economists naively believe that if we "just leave it to the market," everything will turn out wonderfully. The strong will survive, and the weak will perish. Libertarians, meanwhile, believe that *any* restriction on *any* person is an unconscionable violation of sacred rights to private property. "So what if Jeff Bezos gets everything and everyone else gets nothing?" the heartless economist sniffs. "The outcome is *pareto efficient*" (meaning that we can't make anyone else better off without hurting Jeff Bezos). "So what if gun proliferation means mass shootings and criminal mayhem? Owning a gun is my *right*, and you can have my gun when you pry it out of my cold, dead hands." What could one learn from reading the unhinged rantings of such maladjusted sociopaths? And what could they possibly have to say to Christians?

Quite a lot. I reject the strawman versions of economists and libertarians that burn so frequently in the popular press and public discussion. I think the world would be a much better place if critics didn't reject our ideas out of hand. I don't think there is a contradiction between being a libertarian, an economist, and a Christian. The intersection in that Venn diagram might be small, but we do exist, and I think we have something to say. If I may be so bold, whenever someone

3

begins a sentence with "the problem with economics is…", "the problem with libertarianism is…", or "the problem with Christianity is…" they are usually about to say something that shows they haven't thought that much about it and probably don't understand what they're criticizing. If they have eyes to see and just look around a bit, I think they'll see the beauty of economics, the joy of liberty, and the goodness of God in unexpected places. I do daily, and I hope this book of brief reflections will help you do so, too.

# I

# Introduction and Plan of the Work: Let's Look Out the Window

Three observations motivate this collection. First, most of us don't know how societies function. I don't mean at the deep, cultural-and-institutional level where scholars are doing cutting-edge research in the social sciences and humanities. I mean that most of us fundamentally do not understand things as basic as "exchange makes people better off." Second, my beloved dismal science of economics illuminates social mysteries; it helps us understand and navigate the kind of world God created in light of the kind of beings God created. Third, we economists haven't done a good job communicating these principles. We're decent at publicizing the latest research findings. Our students pick up a few interesting and useful ideas in our courses. We are not, however, very good at explaining the *Hidden Order* of a free society, to borrow the title of one of David Friedman's books (Dr. Friedman and his late father, the Nobel Laureate Milton Friedman, are among the exceptions). In over fifteen years of teaching economics and writing commentaries aimed first at myself—do *I* understand this?—and second at students and non-economists, I've thought, "we can do better than this."

That brings us to this book, which collects articles I wrote for AIER from the beginning of 2019 through mid-2020, plus a few other pieces I've written over the years. With an exception or two, each article gets a chapter, a light revision, and maybe a new title. There's a footnote with bibliographic information on the original article whenever a new article appears. I've had to remove hyperlinks, of course. I've worked to limit documentation to actual sources and not *everything* to which I linked in the online articles, and relevant citations appear in a bibliography at the end of the book. I've worked to make the chapters short enough that you can read a chapter waiting to buy milk or read the book waiting to renew your driver's license. The economist Ronald Coase, who won the Nobel Prize in 1991, urged economists to "look out the window" at the world around them. Let's do that.

We can see what Glasgow, Vienna, Chicago, and the other places where economics developed have to do with Athens, but what do they have to do with Jerusalem? Our beloved dismal science studies an emergent and beautiful social order—a market economy—in which we take social miracles for granted. One of the coolest things about studying economics is that you start to appreciate the beauty of an undesigned social order in which billions of independent minds cooperate to mutual advantage. Seeing the social world through the lenses economics provides is like looking at pictures taken with a powerful microscope or a deep space telescope. They almost compel me to worship. The Bible says the heavens declare the glory of God. So do the laws of supply and demand and the quantity theory of money.

In introducing his classic *I, Pencil*, Leonard E. Read of the Foundation for Economic Education quoted GK Chesterton, who said that "We are perishing for want of wonder, not for want of wonders." In a famous clip from Conan O'Brien's show, Louis CK was right: everything's *amazing,* and nobody's happy. Consider the time-honored tradition of complaining about air travel. Flying is *incredible*. One day in the Spring semester of 2019, I taught my Monday classes, went to the airport, flew from Birmingham to Atlanta, flew from Atlanta to Los Angeles, picked up a rental car, drove to Coronado, slept at a hotel, bought some stuff at a Walmart, spoke at La Sierra University, ate a lovely dinner, drove my rental car back to the airport, flew from Los Angeles to Atlanta and then from Atlanta to Birmingham, and taught my Wednesday classes. In about 48 hours, I could teach in Alabama, lecture in California, and then get back in time for classes in Alabama again. It's remarkable, and it's easy to lose sight of at a time when miracles have become mundane.

I hope this book is an exercise in recapturing *wonder,* à la Chesterton, by drawing from day-to-day experience using what the economist Alfred Marshall (again) called "the study of man in the ordinary business of life." It is this "ordinary business" that I find most captivating. I interpret at least my little sliver of God's mandate to "fill the earth and subdue it" as an appeal to try to understand the principles underlying social order—"thinking God's thoughts after Him," as Johannes Kepler put it, but about the social world rather than the physical. I hope *Strangers With Candy* will help us capture a bit more wonder—and perhaps even more importantly, a bit more humility. Christians should undoubtedly do justice and love mercy, but I hope this book and books like it help us walk a little more humbly with our God.

Many readers who disagree with me might reply, "well, *actually*, so-and-so in such-and-such paper shows that under conditions A, B, and C, the intervention you're criticizing makes people better off." Indeed, these are right. When you have a monopsony, price floors might increase gains from trade. When you have a monopoly, price ceilings might increase gains from trade. Theoretically, tariffs *might* make Americans better off. It's possible. I don't think it's probable.

However, in my judgment—and I may very well be very wrong—the critical problem in economics education and economic policy is not that people don't appreciate market failure. They don't appreciate markets. I wrote a lot of what follows to illustrate the fundamentals. So read on. And if you find any particularly egregious mistakes or places where the exposition is especially unclear, email me at art.carden@gmail.com. I'll forever be in your debt as I try to improve next time.

People like big ideas simply and briefly stated. When asked, "which is the great commandment in the Law," Jesus replied, "You shall love the Lord your God with all your heart and with all your soul and with all your mind. This is the great and first commandment. And a second is like it: You shall love your neighbor as yourself. On these two commandments depend all the Law and the Prophets" (Matthew 22:36-40). Rabbi Hillel summarized the Torah while standing on one foot: "that which is hateful to do, don't do to your neighbor. The rest is commentary." Someone once asked Ayn Rand to summarize her philosophy while standing on one foot. Her reply: "metaphysics: objective reality. Epistemology: reason. Ethics: self-interest. Politics: capitalism." In 2011, I made a video for the Institute for Humane Studies. I summarized the basic economic ideas while standing on one foot (and yes, I stood on one foot for every take). The video is a little longer at two minutes and 14 seconds, but Stephen Landsburg sums it up nicely in his book *The Armchair Economist*: "All of economics can be summarized in four words: 'people respond to incentives.' The rest is commentary." I invite you, then, to the following pages of commentary.

# PART I

# Things Have Never Been Better, and There's No Limit on the Horizon

# 2

# The Past is a Nice Place to Visit. You Wouldn't Want to Live There.

I don't think most people appreciate just how much better our world is than the world of our ancestors. Maybe you've heard something like this: "Our modern, industrialized lives are harried, hurried, and confusing. Wouldn't it have been nice to live long ago when things were so much simpler? When people were rooted and connected? When we lived in harmony with one another, nature, and the generations that came before us?"

No. Nostalgia for "the good old days" puzzles me because they were horrible. The past is a fascinating place to visit—while combing through historical records from the comfort of my well-lit, air-conditioned office or my well-lit, air-conditioned living room or a well-lit, air-conditioned coffee shop. I certainly wouldn't want to live there. Having lived through it since about 1979, I wouldn't want to return.

---

Carden, Art. 2019. "The Past Is a Nice Place to Visit. You Wouldn't Want to Live There." *American Institute for Economic Research*. July 18. The chapter draws from Rosling (2018).The original version of the article was also the basis for chapter 5 of McCloskey and Carden (2020).

Note my emphasis on "well-lit." One product of the Enlightenment was literal en*light*enment. As 2018 economics co-Nobelist William Nordhaus (1996) explains, the cost of artificial lighting has been in freefall. Light is so cheap that we remind ourselves and one another to turn the lights off when we leave rooms to conserve energy and protect the environment, not necessarily to save money. Turning the light off when you leave a room is more liturgical than financial: you hit the light switch because it's what good, environmentally-conscious people do.

Contrast this to what Johnny Cash sang about in "Pickin' Time": "It's hard to see by the coal-oil light/and I turn it off pretty early at night/a jug of coal oil costs a dime/but I stay up late come pickin' time." Expensive coal oil and low incomes made light a luxury.

History is a story of literal and figurative darkness. Here's 1993 Nobel Laureate Douglass C. North's assessment from page 7 of his 2005 book *Understanding the Process of Economic Change*:

> "Economic history is a depressing tale of miscalculation leading to famine, starvation, defeat in warfare, death, economic stagnation and decline, and indeed the disappearance of entire civilizations. And even the most casual inspection of today's news suggests that this tale is not purely a historical phenomenon. Yet we do get it right sometimes, as the past few centuries' spectacular economic growth attests. But ongoing success is hardly a foregone conclusion."

Jonah Goldberg puts it this way on page 6 of his 2018 book *Suicide of the West*: "The natural state of mankind is grinding poverty punctuated by horrific violence terminating with an early death. It was like this for a very, very long time."

## The Past is a Nice Place to Visit. You Wouldn't Want to Live There.

Not so any longer. There has never been a better time to be alive. As Deirdre McCloskey (2006, 2010, 2016) argues in her "Bourgeois Era" trilogy, things have never been so good.

Just how good are they? The late Hans Rosling—data virtuoso and TED talker extraordinaire—offered some relevant information in his 2018 book *Factfulness* (which his son and daughter finished after he passed away from pancreatic cancer) that I use in what follows. Rosling explains how important it is to get the facts straight. The facts about our liberalizing world are incredible.

The data give the lie to the "rich get richer, poor get poorer" trope. The world's extreme poverty rate has halved in a matter of decades. Only 9% of the world's population now lives in "low income" countries, and 75% live in "middle income" countries. By 2017, only 9% of the world's population lived on less than $2 a day. That's nine percentage points too many in the view of any decent person, but it's far better than the 85 percent of the world's population living on less than $2 a day in 1800. The change is happening fast enough that these data might change appreciably between when I wrote this and when you read it.

To the extent that this was "a simpler time," it was because grinding, $2-a-day poverty didn't give people a lot of chances to make complex choices. If you didn't scratch the ground hard enough day in and day out, you died. It was as simple as that. Of course, you might have had a better diet and more leisure had you been around before settled agriculture—and had you been fortunate enough to avoid having your head caved in by a rock-wielding member of a rival tribe.

People live a lot longer, even though there are more of us. With higher productivity and medical innovation, we have slain or seriously wounded two horsemen of the apocalypse, famine and plague. Worldwide, life expectancy in 1800 was 31. It had risen to 72 in 2017. People in poor countries today live longer than people in rich countries two centuries ago. Tumbling child mortality is one of the main reasons. In 1800, 44 percent of children died before the age of 5. In 2016, only 4 percent of a much larger population did. Perhaps there's a simple, serene dignity that comes with burying a child or dying in childbirth, but it's a simple, serene dignity my wife and I are happy to forsake.

Our lives are also much healthier and safer (notwithstanding the COVID-19 pandemic). Rosling reports data on 194 countries. One hundred forty-eight of them had smallpox cases in 1850. None did in 1979. There were 453 disaster deaths per million people in the 1930s and only 10 per million between 2010 and 2016, which means that if climate change increases the disaster death rate tenfold, it will *still* be less than a quarter of what it was in the 1930s. In 1980, I was among the lucky 22% of one-year-olds worldwide who got at least one vaccination. That percentage had quadrupled to 88% in 2016.

We can use all this new life and better health to enjoy a broader array of cultural goods. In 1860, there was *one* new music recording. In 2015, there were 6,201,002. There was *one* new feature film in 1906 and 11,000 in 2016. In 1665, there were 119 scholarly articles published, so few that it would have been easy to keep up with new ideas. An Oxford don in 1665 could have read *all* the academic journal articles. In 2016, however, there were 2,550,000. In the 21st century, it is difficult for a scholar to keep up with developments in one's narrow subfield.

It is all *far* more widely available, and it is growing by the minute. What used to be limited to the literate and learned Oxford don is now more widely available to virtually everyone. In 1800, 10 percent of adults worldwide were literate. In 2016, it was 86 percent. Liberal societies, it turns out, have democratized knowledge and brought us out of literal and figurative darkness and into literal and figurative light.

Significantly, music, movies, books, and articles aren't lost, so all these recordings, films, and scholarly articles form the existing cultural capital stock. They don't replace it. That means garage bands and authors face ever-tougher challenges as they have to produce music that's preferable, at the margin, to listening to *Dark Side of the Moon* again and books that are preferable, at the margin, to re-reading a classic or searching the classics for something you haven't read yet.

Should we study and learn from the past? Of course we should. Should we yearn for the past, seek to return there, and perhaps undo the last several centuries' progress? Of course we shouldn't. We live longer, richer, healthier lives with opportunities to flourish that our ancestors couldn't have comprehended. If anything, we should look upon our lot and sing for joy. With 11,000 playable guitars per million people in 2014 compared to only 200 per million people in 1962, I think we're up to the challenge.

Nostalgia for a "simpler time" is misplaced. In 2005, the comic strip "Pearls Before Swine" shows the character Wee Bear trekking across the country to find Willie Mays and urge him to "get back into center field" and unite the country, just as it was in 1957. Willie Mays replies: "back when I couldn't eat in certain restaurants?" Think it possible those densely textured structures of meaning for which you are so nostalgic, whether you are of the left or the right, are simply not all they're cracked up to be.

*All that we are is the result of what we have thought.*
—fortune cookie, July 25, 2019[1]

So we live in a very different world. What explains the differences between *then*, when life for virtually anyone was solitary, poor, nasty, brutish, and short, and *now*, when life is growing more and more connected, wealthy, clean, peaceful, and long for more and more people? There are many explanations for what Goldberg calls "the miracle" of modern, liberal, democratic, capitalist peace and prosperity. As Deirdre McCloskey shows in her 2010 book *Bourgeois Dignity* and her 2016 book *Bourgeois Equality*, most of the usual explanations don't do the entire explanatory job. Railroads and transportation improvements, for example, might account for a few percentage points of the difference between the standards of living Then and Now. They don't get us anywhere close to understanding the ten- to one-hundred-fold increase we want to explain.

If it wasn't material factors like railroads and high savings rates, might it have been property rights and good institutions? Here I depart from McCloskey in that I think institutions and institutional changes are probably more important than she gives them credit for being in her 2010 and 2016 books, but she's right that the timing and geography, for the most part, don't work very well. The rule of law goes back to Hammurabi, and British property rights were as secure and well-enforced in the thirteenth century as in the eighteenth. McCloskey explains how good institutions protecting property rights are necessary but insufficient for the Great Enrichment of the last three centuries.

McCloskey emphasizes *intellectual* change and, specifically, a widespread embrace of innovation. So does Northwestern University's Joel Mokyr—particularly in his 2009 book *The Enlightened Economy: An Economic History of Britain, 1700-1850* and his 2016 book *A Culture of Growth: The Origins of the Modern Economy*. In *The Enlightened Economy*, Mokyr emphasizes "the Industrial Enlightenment." In *A Culture of Growth*, he expands on this theme more generally. He argues that economic progress happened because of an ideological change among European intellectual and moral elites. A common elite language united them (Latin). Bound together by falling postal costs and protected (at least somewhat) by a politically-fragmented Europe where lords, nobles, and rulers courted intellectuals they might have wished to retain as advisors and tutors. Europe's political fragmentation meant the rulers played whack-a-mole with heretics and critics. A noble might try to suppress one thinker's wicked ideas only to see him pop up a few principalities under the protection of a different noble. Heterodox thinkers weren't *completely* safe, but they were safe enough that they started the Enlightenment.

As Mokyr argues, these intellectual and cultural elites came to embrace the idea that progress is *possible* and *desirable*. The Industrial Revolution, therefore, was the outgrowth of these ideas, which were, in turn, the product of a "Republic of Letters" uniting—or at least facilitating conversation between—thinkers scattered across a politically-fragmented Europe. It wasn't that European rulers didn't *try* to suppress the free flow of ideas. They didn't succeed like rulers in other parts of the world.

The fruits of the Enlightenment surround you. "What we have thought" is part of our intellectual and spiritual reality. Our material reality embodies it, too. My computer isn't valuable because of its chemical and material composition but because it incorporates a bewildering array of ideas—things people have thought. The computer made it from a factory to my desk because of what people thought about steel, vulcanized rubber, glass, and internal combustion. An *object* only becomes a *resource* when thought infuses it. In other words, something is only a *resource* if we have figured out how to use it to satisfy our wants. Until ideas transformed them, minerals and oil were just so much dirt and goo.

## 3

# Markets Aren't Magic, But They Are Marvelous

F ree people in free markets enriched the world, and I am, like the 1986 Nobel Laureate James M. Buchanan, a "zealous advocate of the market order" even though I gave up my youthful socialism long before he did. There seems to be something suspicious about free-market economists' insistence that "the free market" can handle just about everything, though. Do libertarian economists like me believe that free markets are inscrutable magic? I have read critics of free markets use words like "sorcery" (in Eugene McCarraher's *The Enchantments of Mammon*) and "magic" and "faith" (in Lawrence Glickman's *Free Enterprise: An American History*). Those who sneer at economics as "faith-based" or "the dismal pseudoscience" make what I think is a crucial mistake: they confuse a statement like "No single person knows how to make a pencil" (true) with "We don't have any idea how markets work, so just have *faith* that they will give us the right outcomes"

---

Carden, Art. 2020. "Do Economists Believe in "Magic"? No, We Believe in Markets." American Institute for Economic Research. April 8.

(false). We have a pretty good idea of how markets work, but we don't appreciate them.

The critics who think economists are sorcerers and con artists are missing the forest for the trees. Those of us who (try to) teach economics know the struggle. As my intermediate micro professor, Akram Temimi, wrote on the board on the first day of class when I took it way back in 1999, and as I regularly remind my students, "economics is *hard*." It's abstract and counterintuitive, and studying it is sometimes a little like watching a magic show. I still remember the "whoa—*no way*" feeling when Dr. Temimi explained welfare economics's fundamental theorems. It seems incredible to suggest that order and prosperity emerge without being consciously and deliberately *planned* by some higher authority. God indirectly gives us our daily bread through cooperation and exchange with others who bear his image.

This is Read's message in "I, Pencil." He illustrates how simple, voluntary exchange leads to social "miracles" like the pencil and a host of other things. Read explains how, to borrow from Adam Smith's contemporary Adam Ferguson, so many of the things we take for granted are the results of human *action* within a framework that respects private property rights and allows voluntary exchange but not the deliberate products of human *design*. Of course, someone *does* design a pencil, but she uses others' knowledge of processes she hasn't learned and doesn't understand. There are many ways to make something you can call a "pencil." Economic calculation using market prices, as Ludwig von Mises explained, shows us the "right" way—that is, the design and production processes that give us pencils without leaving more urgent wants unsatisfied.

In "I, Pencil," Read is stripping away the complications and laying bare the underlying essence of the issue, which I find amazing every time I teach comparative advantage and gains from trade. Specialization and division of labor mean we have consumption possibilities beyond our production possibilities. We get more from the sweat of our brow because we can specialize and exchange.

Here's a simple numerical example. Consider two people: David and Ricardo. They can produce two goods: potatoes and tomatoes. Suppose that in a day, David could grow twelve potatoes or six tomatoes. Ricardo, however, lives on better land that might be especially suitable for tomatoes. Suppose Ricardo can grow *twenty* potatoes or a *hundred* tomatoes in a day.

For simplicity's sake, assume David spends all his time growing potatoes and Ricardo spends all his time growing tomatoes. David eats twelve potatoes a day and no tomatoes. Ricardo eats a hundred tomatoes a day and no potatoes. Then, one day, David offers to trade Ricardo one tomato for one potato. Ricardo accepts the deal.

Here is where the "magic" happens. I put "magic" in quotation marks because it isn't *actually* magic, of course, and we *do* understand it pretty well. That doesn't mean it isn't incredible. Instead of twelve potatoes and no tomatoes, David now gets eleven potatoes and a single tomato from the sweat of his brow. Ricardo's labor now bears 99 tomatoes and one potato.

That doesn't seem remarkable until you ask what David would have given up to get a tomato if Ricardo weren't there. Remember David's production possibilities—twelve potatoes or six tomatoes—and where he started—twelve potatoes and no tomatoes. Had he wanted to grow a tomato on his own, it would have cost him the opportunity to grow two potatoes (12/6=2, so each tomato costs him two potatoes). If he had switched entirely from potato production to tomato production, he would have given up twelve potatoes to get six tomatoes. If he decided to grow a tomato on his own, he would only enjoy ten potatoes and one tomato rather than the eleven potatoes and one tomato he could enjoy because he could trade. In this example, growing a tomato would have cost him two potatoes. Because he can trade with

Ricardo, each tomato only costs a single potato. His daily "bread" with trade—eleven potatoes and one tomato—would have been impossible to achieve independently.

Since David is better off, he has taken advantage of Ricardo, right? Wrong, and here again is a crucial point: David makes himself better off *by making Ricardo better off too*. Ricardo went from 100 tomatoes and zero potatoes to 99 tomatoes and one potato. What if Ricardo hadn't had the opportunity to trade with David and had decided to grow his own potato?

If he switched completely from tomatoes to potatoes, he would give up 100 tomatoes for 20 potatoes, so each potato would cost him five tomatoes. *With* trade, Ricardo enjoys 99 tomatoes and one potato. *Without* trade, the best he could do was 95 tomatoes and one potato. Ricardo's daily "bread" with trade—99 tomatoes and one potato—*would have been impossible to achieve on his own*—just like David. Without trade, each tomato would cost David 2 potatoes. With trade, each tomato only costs David 1 potato. Without trade, each potato would cost Ricardo 5 tomatoes. With trade, each potato costs Ricardo only one tomato.

The rest, they say, is economics: the entire dismal science rests on this simple insight: specialization makes our labor more productive. We could complicate this in all sorts of different ways, which happens when we move from specialization to supply and demand.

The contexts and settings become more complicated, but the essential insight—that specialization and exchange give us more of what we value—doesn't change. This simple example blows up the notions so popular among those who denounce economics as "sorcery" that there is only so much stuff to go around, that all of history is a story of class struggle, and that the only way for Ricardo to be one of the *Haves* is for David to be one of the *Have Nots*.

Our critics also overlook an essential lesson. Exchange helps us share knowledge. David, the expert potato cultivator, can use the knowledge of Ricardo, the expert tomato cultivator. David doesn't need to know the finer points of the care and feeding of tomatoes. Ricardo doesn't need to know the finer points of the care and feeding of potatoes. Friedrich Hayek referred to this as "the knowledge of the particular circumstances of time and place." Exchange allows David to harness and deploy tomato-growing expertise he doesn't have himself.

"This might be all well and good in theory," you might be saying, "and I'm sure it works nicely in the context of your very abstract classroom example—but when do we see this in the real world?" My answer: pretty much any time you do anything. Earlier this morning, the guy who rakes our yard came by. Because he specializes in leaf-raking, I can write more economics articles. In just a little bit, I'm going to make lunch. Is it free, or even cheap? It isn't: making lunch takes time, so I'm giving up the opportunity to do something. My wife baked a lot of bread early in the Covid-19 pandemic. Was this cheaper than getting it from the store or a bakery? It wasn't: fresh, warm, homemade bread is quite a treat, but it's expensive—not unlike the tomatoes for which David would have to sacrifice a princely *two* potatoes if he couldn't buy them from Ricardo.

I occasionally wax rhapsodic in the classroom because I think economics is beautiful. I find it especially interesting that many problems have the same logical structure. As I recall how Hoover Institution economist John Cochrane put it, it's remarkable how many can be explained and understood using supply and demand when you think hard about them. Determination of wages in competitive markets? Supply and demand. Loanable funds? Supply and demand. Insurance? Supply and demand. Education? Supply and demand. Religion? Supply and demand. Broccoli? Supply and demand. Pornography? Supply and demand. Obviously, the problems differ in their details, but they share an underlying logical structure. And I, like Cochrane, find that remarkable.

# 4

# The Self-Interest of Strangers Can Lead to a Symphony of Creation

Blanche Dubois, the anti-heroine of Tennessee Williams' *A Streetcar Named Desire*, was a woman of many mistakes who depended on the kindness of strangers. People strive to be more decent than we might initially expect, even though they are also capable of unspeakable horrors. Nonetheless, it is far more reliable to depend not on their kindness but on their self-interest.

Why is this? For all of our bluster about universal brotherhood and imagining all the people sharing and living life in peace, people have limited capacity for benevolence and even more limited knowledge of what Friedrich Hayek (1945) called "the particular circumstances of time and place" that other people meet in their *local* situations. In *Suicide of the West,* Jonah Goldberg recounts a vivid example in which former Senator Phil Gramm—the father of my former department chair Marshall Gramm at Rhodes College—told an audience that,

---

Carden, Art. 2019. "The Market Is a Symphony of Creation" American Institute for Economic Research. November 26.

quite simply, no one could love his children the way he and his wife could. Someone in the audience replied, "that's not true! I love them as much as you do!"

Gramm replied: "What are their names?"

That kind of quick wit ended the argument and made Gramm's point. We can't *love* strangers in much more than an abstract sense, and to equate this to other kinds of love is a bit of a betrayal of the concept, as C.S. Lewis explains it in *The Four Loves*. Moreover, the nasty social media antics of "the woke" betray the ideas of peace and brotherhood. Satire website The Babylon Bee has captured this perfectly in spoof articles with titles like "Powerful: Protester writes 'Tolerance' on Face of Man He Just Beat Unconscious" and "Liberal Activist Explains Notion Of Tolerance To Man She Just Called A 'Worthless [Expletive].'" It's a curious brand of love, perhaps suitable for the Ministry of Love in George Orwell's *1984*.

The simple problem is that people don't know strangers well enough to love them like they love friends and family. Adam Smith was clear in a famous passage in *The Wealth of Nations*. He explained how we *never talk* to the butcher, the baker, and the brewer about our needs but of their advantages. The point bears repeating: the butcher has his own family, friends, wants, desires, hopes, and dreams. Respect for his autonomy and agency dictates that we not expect him to forsake those for our sake. Coercion violates Immanuel Kant's appeal to treat one another not as *means* to our ends but as ends unto themselves.

If you want people to help you, it's wise to give them a reason to. Offer a better deal than the next person, and you will have what you want. Note that this doesn't make any assumptions about what people should want or how they should act. It assumes that they have preferences and plans—and those preferences and plans need to be respected.

Here's a pedestrian example from the day our youngest child had a tonsillectomy—when people who do not love him like I do cared for him like I cannot. I ate a delicious sandwich at the hospital. It was called the blue river brisket, and it had brisket, cheddar cheese, bacon, purple slaw, garlic mayo, and barbecue sauce heated and served on a kaiser roll. I had it with a bowl of broccoli cheddar soup. It was a perfect meal on a dreary and stressful day.

The soup and sandwich were probably not the best things I could've eaten in the long run. In the short run, however, it was excellent comfort food. The remarkable fact is that so many people conspired to provide me with a delicious sandwich and a delicious bowl of soup even though they don't know me; they don't know the circumstances under which I wanted the sandwich and a bowl of soup and, while I'm sure they care about my son in some abstract sense, they don't love him like I do or like they love their friends and family.

The free(-ish) market directed their concern for themselves and their loved ones so that the best way they could take care of them was to care for my family and me on a very stressful morning. The ladies who made the sandwich and the soup don't know me from Adam, and while I'm sure they are concerned about my son in an abstract sense, I doubt they lost sleep wondering how my son was recovering.

A lot of other people were involved, as well. I paid for the meal using Apple Pay, which automatically charged it to my Amazon Visa card. There are a lot of people involved in the programming of the software that makes Apple Pay work and a lot of people involved in the manufacture of my iPhone who again probably don't care very specifically about my family but who are nonetheless helping to bear my burden because of the incentives they face in sort-of-free markets.

The bread, the beef, the cheddar cheese, the barbecue sauce, the slaw, and the soup ingredients all had to get to the hospital-lobby café somehow. Somewhere, there's a truck driver who will never read this article and who might, if anything, have open contempt for my family and me should they get to know us who helped us during our hour of need by getting sandwich ingredients from the source to the café. The people who baked the bread, the people who grew the wheat that became the bread, and the people who served breakfast to the farmers who grew and harvested the wheat all helped me have a delicious meal on a stressful morning.

The market is a symphony of creation, but it is also a symphony of care. In a free market, people can care for one another without necessarily caring about one another. Some people might see this is as a bug rather than a feature. In light of our moral and cognitive limitations—we have a limited ability to have close friends, for example—I find it remarkable that exchange allows us to secure the services of others with knowledge and talent we don't have.

The Bible tells us to bear one another's burdens. I've long wondered exactly how we discharged this duty. It is obvious when talking about people who are close to moral proximity. When a friend or neighbor has a baby, you take them a casserole. Or you give them a gift card for baby wipes or something like that. When someone you know and love is caught short, you put a few dollars in the collection plate and help them.

These ways of bearing one another's burdens are immediate and visible. There are many non-immediate and difficult-to-see ways that we bear one another's burdens even when those others are not in close moral proximity to us. If you have an insurance policy, you are part of a network of people bearing others' burdens. If you're filling out a purchasing order for kaiser rolls for the café in a hospital lobby, you're bearing other people's burdens. If you're making a delicious sandwich, you might bear a hefty burden for the person on the other side of the cash register.

Free markets, of course, have a lot of things going for them. They deliver the goods. We are healthier and wealthier because of what the economist William Baumol called "The Free Market Innovation

Machine." One of the underappreciated attributes of free markets is that we can bear one another's burdens.

Many people that do not know me, probably wouldn't like me if we ever met, and might roll their eyes at the suggestion that we bear one another's burdens in a free market. Nonetheless, they helped me during a bit of a rough patch. And though I may never meet them, I will always be grateful.

**5**

# A Mundane Miracle: Recorded Music

There must be limits to this, right? Economic growth can't continue *forever*, can it? The absurd diffusion of recorded popular music is part of the change. Cooperation with strangers has radically democratized artistic achievement. An authentic, hundred-year-old Edison phonograph is one of the treasures at the American Institute for Economic Research. My family and I spent a few weeks in residence in 2019 and 2020. My kids enjoyed turning the hand crank that got the phonograph going and dancing around the room to the old music. I enjoyed dancing with them and thinking about the radical break with the past and the radical democratization of music the Edison phonograph represented.

It illustrates what the economist Joseph Schumpeter calls "the capitalist achievement" in his classic *Capitalism, Socialism, and Democracy*:

> There are no doubt some things available to the modern workman that Louis XIV himself would have been delighted to have

---

Carden, Art. 2019. "The Capitalist Achievement of Recorded Music." American Institute for Economic Research. July 17.

yet was unable to have—modern dentistry for instance. On the whole, however, a budget on that level had little that really mattered to gain from capitalist achievement. Even speed of traveling may be assumed to have been a minor consideration for so very dignified a gentleman. Electric lighting is no great boon to anyone who has money enough to buy a sufficient number of candles and to pay servants to attend to them. It is the cheap cloth, the cheap cotton and rayon fabric, boots, motorcars, and so on that are the typical achievements of capitalist production, and not as a rule improvements that would mean much to the rich man. Queen Elizabeth owned silk stockings. The capitalist achievement does not typically consist in providing more silk stockings for queens but in bringing them within the reach of factory girls in return for steadily decreasing amounts of effort.

Or, in the musical context, the capitalist achievement consists not of softer seats at the opera for the king and queen but access to a practically infinite library for pennies a day.

Suppose you were a king, a noble, an aristocrat, a Rockefeller, or a Carnegie. You could've hired a private orchestra when you wanted to hear music or brought in the world's greatest comedian for a personal performance when you wanted a laugh. The invention and diffusion of recorded music was revolutionary for people of more modest means who would have had to make music themselves or do without. The phonograph opened a new world to people who could listen to any kind of music from the comfort of their own homes.

The capitalist achievement is progressive downward diffusion of things the rich and privileged take for granted. Consider the iPod. "A thousand songs in your pocket" seemed impossible when it appeared. Now it seems quaint. I bought my first iPod in 2007 and thought it would go down as the early 21st century's iconic gizmo. After all, I could carry thousands of songs and download videos (like TED Talks, with which I quickly became enamored) just by connecting it to my laptop. I was wrong about the iPod, though, as the smartphone quickly superseded it. Now I take it for granted that everyone carries a pocket communicator/encyclopedia/camera/music player/video player/you name it. It doesn't slice or dice, but since you can use it to order a meal and have it delivered within minutes with a few flicks of your thumb, you don't need it to.

The world is super-saturated with opportunities to listen to music and watch movies. A few hundred years ago, I would have had to be a king or queen with an orchestra charged with keeping my friends and me entertained. More recently, I would have had to learn how to play the piano. The Edison phonograph and the innovations that came after it made it easier for anyone to listen to just about any kind of music from home. Now, all I need to do is tell my phone to play "Old Town Road," and it happens. It's yet another way the free market helps us live like kings.

Naturally, nothing good comes along without an interest group to oppose it. Recorded music was no different. Calestous Juma devotes a chapter of his excellent book *Innovation and Its Enemies* to opposition to recorded music. It would take the jobs of live musicians, of course, and there is an interesting legal and philosophical question about the right to use and re-use a recording of someone else's artwork. The fear that recorded music would kill live music was overblown, though. As Gill A. Pratt points out, "No one proudly wears T-shirts declaring when they listened to a recorded song." Recorded music can be a gateway to live music, as one might hear at Tanglewood, the Boston Symphony Orchestra's summer home.

At a time when people are enraged because the golden-egg-laying capitalist goose doesn't distribute the eggs in a way they find beautiful, it's worth stepping back and considering just what liberal, capitalist, in-it-for-the-money, free market societies have done and for whose benefit.

The Edison phonograph helped make Thomas Edison a household name. iTunes and the iPod, and the iPhone made Steve Jobs a legend. Amazon has made Jeff Bezos the richest man in the world. The biggest winners from the market's perennial gales of creative destruction haven't been Edison, Jobs, and Bezos. They've been ordinary people like you and me who can simply tell Siri, Alexa, or Google what we want to hear.

A big deal for royalty? Not really. Life-changing for the rest of us? You bet. And it's a clear illustration of how we can use strangers' minds in a market economy.

As you've seen, this is the most fantastic time to be alive, ever. Innovation has democratized music pretty radically. There is a variation from day to day, but I don't think anyone can seriously doubt that the average person's life has improved by leaps and bounds in just the last few centuries. That's all fine and dandy, of course, but aren't there limits?

Nope. Contrary to what many commentators believe, I think there is no actual limit to economic progress.

Before I proceed, I should probably define what I mean by economic *progress* as distinct from economic *growth*. Economic *growth* just means "more stuff." Economic *progress*, meanwhile, as discussed by Randall Holcombe in his 2007 book *Entrepreneurship and Economic Progress*, is the progressive production and accumulation of *better* stuff. It allows people to flourish in ways undreamt of by previous generations.

I think it is unlimited. I draw at least some inspiration from the economist Julian Simon, one of the twentieth century's great minds. Sadly, he passed away in 1998 at the age of 68. His legacy lives on in his book *The Ultimate Resource* and the follow-on volumes it inspired—Matt Ridley's *The Rational Optimist*, for example, Ronald Bailey's *The*

*End of Doom,* and Pierre Desrochers and Joanna Szurkmak's *Population Bombed!* are three recent examples—and the Julian Simon Award bestowed annually by the Competitive Enterprise Institute.

Simon, who was for a long time a professor of business at the University of Maryland, is most notable for his exhaustive and painstaking data collection on long-run trends in resource prices that led him to an important, and I think Nobel Prize-worthy, conclusion: the human mind is the ultimate resource. Necessity being the mother of invention, pressure on the available stock of natural resources will induce people to do two things. First, they will look for new sources. They may dig deeper for oil or various metals, and with the deepest mines on earth coming in at "only" about two miles compared to an average thickness of the earth's crust at some twenty-plus miles, we have only scratched the surface of the planet. Second, they will look for substitutes for these resources and ways of using them. Adjustments might include oil, wind, solar, and nuclear energy or the development of new technologies that allow us to get the same (literal, in this case) bang from a given amount of crude petroleum.

He argued that innovation and substitution make prices fall in the long run. Not everyone agrees, of course, and Simon is probably most notable for a famous bet he made with *Population Bomb* author Paul Ehrlich. In his 1968 book, Ehrlich predicted that millions of people would starve to death in the 1970s because of overpopulation. Instead, we got the Green Revolution, and India became a net grain *exporter*. Undeterred, Ehrlich went on with his gloomy predictions. After sparring with Ehrlich in print for years, Simon finally proposed a bet. They settled on these terms: they would track the inflation-adjusted value of $200 worth of five different commodities—they chose copper, chromium, nickel, tungsten, and tin—for ten years. At the end of the period, they would see what happened to the commodities' prices, and the loser would pay the difference between the settlement price and $1000. Paul

Ehrlich's wife Anne wrote a check for $576.07 because the commodities' prices had fallen by almost sixty percent.

In fairness to Ehrlich—and in acknowledging Simon's understanding of the limitations of the Bet—Ehrlich would have won over several different periods or if they had used a different basket of commodities. He was less careful than this, though, when he actually made the bet, and again, the long-run trends broadly support Simon's thesis that when we bump up against resource constraints, we find ways to innovate around them. And not by accident, either.

# 6

# Turn That Racket Down! Music and Economic Progress

"Economic growth *simply must* stop," you hear the critic saying. Limits to growth are a matter of mathematics: you cannot have unlimited growth in a closed system." I disagree. There may be a fixed number of fundamental particles in the universe and a (large) limit on the number of ways to combine them. Still, these particles aren't all there is to economic progress. As long as we can develop new ways to tell stories and make music, we will have new ways to enjoy life. Consider the musical mini-revolution that happened late in my teenage years when "electronica" took the world by storm. New musical technologies meant new innovators and new ways to make music. They also encouraged members of the musical old guard to try new things.

One of the most notable acts of that era was the Prodigy. Keith Flint, their lead vocalist, passed away on March 4, 2019. Merely by coincidence, I had been listening to their iconic 1997 album, *The Fat of the*

---

Carden, Art. 2019. "How Keith Flint Demonstrated that There are No Limits to Progress." American Institute for Economic Research. March 5.

*Land,* frequently in the weeks before Flint's death. The album was part of a revolution in music that touched the likes of U2 and the Rolling Stones. *The Fat of the Land* came out about three months after U2's *Pop* and three months before the Stones' *Bridges to Babylon.* It's one in a never-ending series of examples of why I don't believe there are meaningful limits to economic progress.

First, when people talk about "limits to economic growth," they often mean "limits to material production." Economic growth, however, means much more than material production. It encompasses everything that makes life worth living, from material goods like TVs to services like haircuts to the arts.

Limits to material production probably don't exist. The possibility of *material* superabundance is a good place to start thinking about artistic (specifically musical) superabundance. Consider the number of ways you can shuffle a simple deck of 52 cards. There are 80,658,175,170,9 43,878,571,660,636,856,403,766,975,289,505,440,883,277,824,000,0 00,000,000 permutations of 52 cards. By comparison, approximately 432,300,000,000,000,000 seconds have elapsed since the beginning of the universe. Suppose you did nothing but shuffle cards once a second. You would get through a fraction of a fraction of a fraction of a fraction of the possibilities before the sun burns out.

That's just a single deck of cards. Now consider that there are about 2,400,000,000,000,000,000,000,000,000,000,000,000,000,000,000,0 00,000,000,000,000,000,000,000,000,000,000 atoms in the universe. That is an incomprehensibly large number that produces an even more incomprehensibly large number of possible combinations. And this isn't even beginning to consider the number of possible locations of all of these combinations. "But we only have one planet!" Fine. Let's take 100,000,000,000,000,000,000,000,000,000,000,000,000,000, 000,000 as the number of atoms on earth.[2] The combinations you can make from that number is perhaps less incomprehensibly large, but it's still incomprehensibly large.

Here's the thing, though: musicians combine sounds, not atoms. There might be an upper limit to the number of possible combinations of sounds out there. A quick Google search suggests that there are more than 5 trillion chords available to a single two-handed pianist and over 42.8 quintillion chords open to two two-handed pianists with an 88-key piano, and this is just music at its most basic.[3] We haven't even begun talking about the possible chord sequences, how musicians can arrange them, or instruments that can accompany the piano.

A hilarious YouTube video by an Australian comedy band called Axis of Awesome mashes up a shocking number of pop songs that follow the same chord progression, from Elton John's "Can You Feel the Love Tonight" to the Beatles' "Let it Be" to A-ha's "Take On Me" to John Denver's "Country Roads" to U2's "With or Without You" to Avril Lavigne's "Complicated" to Offspring's "Self-Esteem" to Lady Gaga's "Poker Face" to "Auld Lang Syne." A lot of popular music is, I will readily admit, absolute garbage that, when set next to Bach or Beethoven, makes me feel like I've been eating from a slop trough when a fine, rare steak awaits me just indoors. The songs they mash up, however, have meant a lot to millions and millions of people who know the sheer and unmitigated joy of belting out the chorus to "Don't Stop Believin'" when it plays on the radio or in the karaoke bar.

Was electronica music? Were the oversexed four-chord pop jingles lampooned by Axis of Awesome really *music*? Beauty is in the eye—or ear—of the beholder, but groups like The Prodigy, Underworld, The Chemical Brothers, Nine Inch Nails, and many others took advantage of new technology and developed new ways of making music—or noise, depending on your preferences. There is no end to the songs we can sing.

# 7

# Slinging Webs in the Unlimited Creative Spider-Verse

There is also no limit to the number of ways people can retell stories. *Spider-Man: Into the Spider-Verse* is a visually stunning example: I'm happy I saw it on the big screen while I had the chance, but it's also great on the small screen.

It's an excellent story that packs complexity and character development into a tidy two-hour runtime. It contains a lot of nice touches I noticed on a second viewing—look at the shape of Dr. Octavius' glasses, for example. The main character, Miles Morales, goes from "geeky, overwhelmed, fumbling teenager" to "new Spider-Man" tightly and convincingly. He's well-positioned for the almost-inevitable run of sequels.

Morales isn't a brand-new character: he made his first appearance in an alternate Spider-Man universe in 2011, and the other Spideys in the movie (Spider-Man Noir, Spider-Ham, Peni Parker & SP//dr,

---

Carden, Art. 2019. "The Unending Creativity of the Spider-Verse." American Institute for Economic Research. April 24.

Spider-Gwen) are from parts of the Spider-Verse I only know because of *Into the Spider-Verse* and what turned up on Wikipedia.

*Into the Spider-Verse* gives the lie to fears about "the end" of economic progress. There is no end to the stories we can tell. There is no end to the ways to reimagine them. As more of our material wants are satisfied, we will likely consume more services, experiences, and stories.

"Reimagine and reboot" has a long and venerable history in the arts. How many different ways have people reimagined Shakespeare? The Leonardo DiCaprio and Claire Danes version of *Romeo and Juliet* (*Romeo + Juliet*) was set in 1990s Southern California. In 2012, the Royal Shakespeare Company set *Julius Caesar* in modern Africa. Ian McKellen has been in a movie adaptation of Richard III set in a fascist, Nazi-esque Britain. Patrick Stewart has been in an adaptation of *Macbeth* set in communist eastern Europe. If Shakespeare is malleable, Spider-Man can be, too.

*Into the Spider-Verse* leaves a casual viewer like me with a lot of questions. What is the Kingpin's backstory in this universe? Has Dr. Octavius told him about cellular degeneration when people switch universes? Does he care? Does *she* care? Does Kingpin in this universe care about what he might do to Kingpin in a different universe? Might he fear reprisal? What's the history between Aunt May and Dr. Octavius? Commentators have pointed out that Octavius says, "My friends actually call me 'Liv'; my *enemies* call me 'Doc Ock'"; and later, when she arrives at Aunt May's house, Aunt May says, "Oh great, it's *Liv*."

The film's profitability tells filmmakers that there's a pretty substantial market for Spider-Man reimaginings. The studios will keep making movies for as long as the benefits from doing so exceed the costs, and as one might expect, a sequel and a few spin-offs are in the works. Embracing the multiverse hypothesis is an interesting move, too, as I think it will allow fans to enjoy spin-off stories without necessarily worrying about how they will affect their preferred timelines. Who knows? Maybe a future *Star Wars* prequel trilogy will tell a different set of stories and banish the 1999/2002/2005 prequel trilogy to a galaxy far, far away in a different universe. In that, I'm just speculating—but if you want to pretend the *Star Wars* prequel trilogy never happened, go right ahead. It's a fictional universe—though my inner child does relish the idea that there does exist some universe in which *Star Wars* and *Spider-Man* happened.

There is also a useful lesson about status and hierarchy that's most evident from one of my favorite installments of the webcomic **XKCD**. It uses plastic crazy-straw design as an example: "Human subcultures are nested fractally. There's no bottom." For better or for worse, people crave status. We measure ourselves by clicks, followers, likes, salary, and so on.

Infinite ways to tell endless stories also imply infinite fandoms and sub-fandoms and sub-sub-fandoms with many opportunities to achieve high status within a little niche. Everyone in academia is familiar with this. We have our heroes and the people we revere—I remember going full fanboy when I first met Walter Williams—about whom no one else cares. I sometimes wonder how many people have sat on planes next to some of my intellectual heroes and influences (Douglass North, Vernon Smith, Elinor Ostrom, Thomas Sowell) and not known that their seatmate is a Very Big Deal.

As communities proliferate, opportunities for status increase. If you use your imagination, I'm sure you can think of several communities you belong to. You have a relatively high status in some and a relatively low status in others. Would it be better if people weren't so status-oriented? I think so, but expanding opportunities for status in a commercial society is an OK second-best.

Innovations in arts and entertainment are constant reminders of our limitless ingenuity and potential. The fear that economic growth *has* to end runs aground on the simple fact that we have endless stories and infinite ways to tell them.

The limitless Spider-Verse is just one example. So long as there are new ways to think about the conflict between someone bitten by a radioactive spider, a crime lord who has lost his family, and a mad scientist with mechanical tentacles, there will be room for economic progress.

# 8

# Ho-Hum. Guess I'll Play Chess With A Stranger on the Other Side of the World.

My favorite passage in Adam Smith comes from *The Theory of Moral Sentiments*. Smith describes a character he calls "the man of system:"

"The man of system, on the contrary, is apt to be very wise in his own conceit; and is often so enamoured with the supposed beauty of his own ideal plan of government, that he cannot suffer the smallest deviation from any part of it. He goes on to establish it completely and in all its parts, without any regard either to the great interests, or to the strong prejudices which may oppose it. He seems to imagine that he can arrange the different members of a great society with as much ease as the hand arranges the different pieces upon a chess-board. He does not consider that the pieces upon the chess-board have no other principle of motion besides that which the hand impresses upon them; but

---

Carden, Art. 2020. "Managing the Chessboard of Human Society: Lessons from the Online Chessboard." American Institute for Economic Research. June 19.

that, in the great chess-board of human society, every single piece has a principle of motion of its own, altogether different from that which the legislature might choose to impress upon it. If those two principles coincide and act in the same direction, the game of human society will go on easily and harmoniously, and is very likely to be happy and successful. If they are opposite or different, the game will go on miserably, and the society must be at all times in the highest degree of disorder."

I thought about that a lot more during the COVID-19 pandemic, roughly right around the time our semester ended. I abandoned social media and took up chess. I have a lot of room for improvement, to put it mildly. As I commented during one online tournament in which I participated, "Watching my king during end games is like watching the weak gazelle that got separated from the pack in a nature documentary." I imagine David Attenborough narrating one of my games and weeping. In *The Art of War*, Sun-Tzu writes "He wins his battles by making no mistakes. Making no mistakes is what establishes the certainty of victory, for it means conquering an enemy that is already defeated." Let's just say Sun-Tzu probably wouldn't be very impressed with my performance.

As I've spent more time honing my skills at the world's greatest game, I've spent a fair bit of time thinking about what the actual chessboard and the emerging culture surrounding it might be teaching us about the supposed chessboard of human society. I work to notice the seemingly miraculous in the mundane, and it's surprising how much we can see in a "simple" game with thirty-two pieces on sixty-four squares. All in all, it illustrates the futility of thinking we can create a master plan for society. Here are some observations based on what I've seen during my short time in the growing world of online chess. I remain convinced that there are no limits to economic progress, and online chess provides another illustration.

### Ho-Hum. Guess I'll Play Chess With A Stranger on the Other Side of the World.

Chess is a deceptively simple game. Each piece moves a certain way—it has a "law of motion" described by the game's rules. Easy-peasy. The elegance and seeming simplicity of chess, however, mask its complexity. According to the great information theorist Claude Shannon, there are $10^{40}$ possible chess positions and $10^{120}$ possible chess games. This post provides interesting commentary, analysis, and criticism, but if we're within a few dozen orders of magnitude of the "real" answer, we're still dealing with an incomprehensibly large number. About 436 quadrillion seconds have passed since the Big Bang. If people have played a trillion different chess games per second since the Big Bang, you would still need to multiply that number by ten about another hundred times before you've played the number of possible games. A trillion games a second since the Big Bang would be about 0.000000000000000000000000000000000000000000000000000000000000000000000000000000000000000000000000000436% of possible games. It's such an amazingly tiny number that if I'm missing a few zeroes—or have added a few extra—it doesn't change the larger point that this is a space we will almost certainly never explore thoroughly. If everyone in the world devoted all of their time to nothing but chess, we still might not exhaust all the possible games before the heat death of the universe.

And chess is just *one game*. To worry about limits to economic progress is like worrying that we will run out of combinations of sounds and exhaust all musical possibilities. When we think about this in the context of the chess set, a single chess set or any other board game means practically infinite possibilities. In *Jurassic Park*, Jeff Goldblum's character, a mathematician named Ian Malcolm, famously says, "life finds a way." So do innovation and economic progress.

Before the COVID-19 pandemic practically stopped the world in its tracks, one of my students asked how people earn their livings streaming themselves playing video games on Twitch.tv might affect GDP and employment numbers. I think it will be quite some time before Twitch streaming and YouTube are big enough to make much of a difference in employment and GDP statistics, but they illustrate a much larger process. It would be a mistake to think that a few thousand people watching a Twitch.tv stream of a chess match portends some sort of large-scale revolution; that's still only a few tenths of a percentage point of the 15.8 million or so people who watch the average NFL game.

It's just as bad a mistake, though, to look to one big thing to save us all. Innovation creates new possibilities, though, and necessity is the mother of invention. The surge in popularity of game streaming and online chess shows how people soften the blow when big adverse shocks hit. Twitch.tv chess streaming and youtube videos of people playing Minecraft are not revolutionary by themselves. They are, however, illustrative of a much larger social process. They are drops in what Don Boudreaux (2016) calls "The Prosperity Pool." They are unremarkable by themselves—if online chess streaming disappeared tomorrow, it wouldn't hurt me that much—but again, they are small parts of a much larger process that has led, over time, to standards of living our ancestors couldn't have imagined. Could they have played chess? Of course. Could they have played a thousand games in a couple of months with people worldwide and gotten instructions and insights from some of the world's best players? Probably not.

One of the simple pleasures of watching elite performers in any venture is to see the absolute mastery of something very difficult. The gymnast Simone Biles, for example, seems superhuman. The world's best chess players are scattered across the globe, from the United States (Fabiano Caruana and Hikaru Nakamura) to Norway (Magnus Carlsen) to Russia (Peter Svidler and Daniil Dubov) to Iran (Alireza Firouzja) to Holland via Russia (Anish Giri), just to name a few places. In following tournaments on Chess24 I've enjoyed the banter between Lawrence Trent (England), Jan Gustaffson (Germany), Laurent Fressinet (France), and others. Someone in Croatia hosts the most popular chess YouTube channel. It looks pretty easy to hire a chess coach from around the world at a reasonable hourly rate. When you play online, you're getting matched up against people from around the world. It would be a worse world in every sense if we had to ask government permission before letting chess moves or ideas cross international borders.

Chess itself is a global game with a global history. It started in India, migrated to Persia, and spread around the world. The word "checkmate," I learned from an interview with Alireza Firouja, comes from *shah mat*, which is "Persian for 'the king is helpless.'"[4] Indeed, the very process of writing this has been an exercise in decentralized, unplanned global cooperation (Wikipedia, HJR Murray's 1913 *The History of Chess*, available for $0 and downloadable on Google Books, the laptop on which I'm writing a Google Doc). I shudder to think about what we have lost because people have insisted so frequently on violently interposing themselves between two others who wish to cooperate.

In my quest to get better at chess and experiment with online learning, I bought a premium membership to Chess24.com. I wouldn't know their home base without looking it up, but consider everything going on here. I paid a company run by people I'll probably never meet living in a part of the world I may never visit. The transactions were processed and recorded instantly by PayPal. Soon, another automatic transaction will send funds from my bank account to PayPal. While someone along the line may abscond with my money—and things like that have happened to me—it's simply astonishing that such things happen so infrequently given the sheer volume of transactions occurring at any time.

Competition is a much more effective check on scumbaggery than people usually think, and this is one of the crucial insights economics brings to the table. Even if we assume a world peopled with selfish sociopaths, we can still get a surprising degree of cooperation just because of the incentives people face. If I'm unhappy with my experience on a chess site or with a payment processor, it's not that hard to take my business elsewhere. As M. Todd Henderson and Salen Churi point out in their book *The Trust Revolution*, innovations in the provision of trust and assurance are substitutes for the regulators. Uber, they argue, competes not with taxi companies but with the taxi commission.

Mundane examples about something as seemingly trivial as a board game should make us pause and be a little more humble about our ability to plan society. They illustrate the point F.A. Hayek made in *The Fatal Conceit*:

> "The curious task of economics is to demonstrate to men how little they really know about what they imagine they can design. To the naive mind that can conceive of order only as the product of deliberate arrangement, it may seem absurd that in complex conditions order, and adaptations to the unknown, can be achieved more efficiently by decentralizing decisions and that a division of authority will actually extend the possibility of overall order. Yet that decentralization actually leads to more information being taken into account."

The Bible tells us to be faithful in small things to be trusted with much. I think there's a clear lesson from my experience of playing chess online. It seems reasonable that we will never master every possible detail of chess, Monopoly, and other games. If games that happen within very well-defined spaces according to very well-defined rules present such insurmountable difficulties, I'm skeptical of the notion that we can design and control a great society.

# PART II

# Lending Strangers a Helping (Invisible) Hand

# 9

# How to Talk to Strangers: Adam Smith and the Invisible Hand

I get a lot of my skepticism about planning and government intervention from Adam Smith. To read Smith is to be almost overwhelmed with the conviction that you have wasted your life. Smith is difficult, but he is not difficult because he is opaque or imprecise, as is the case with so many academic scribblers past and present. He is difficult because he is profound, in every sentence and with every word. Smith is worth engaging. He doesn't assume a prominent place in the core curriculum at every institution of higher learning, and this is a tragedy.

The public mind associates Smith with business, capitalism, and "conservative" economics. Smith was no friend of the businessman. Thomas Sowell noted that you don't spend ten years writing a nine-hundred-page book to say how satisfied you are with the status quo. You only do that if *something* is bugging you. In the commercial sphere, the principles conservatives seek to "conserve" are, in fact, quite radical: the idea that we

---

Carden, Art. 2016. "Why Read Adam Smith." Intercollegiate Studies Institute. January 6.

have *by right* the liberty and dignity to buy low and sell high—and most important, to say "no thank you" to someone's offer—was and is quite radical. And as our history demonstrates, we still haven't quite got it right. Smith had no patience for special pleading. He was wary of businesspeople's motives, noting that they don't gather even for amusement before the conversation turns into a conspiracy against the public.

Smith understood, more than two centuries before James Buchanan won the Nobel Prize for developing the field, some of the basic tenets of public choice theory. He argued that we should be skeptical of calls from merchants and traders to protect or regulate their businesses in the name of the public interest, for it was quite remarkable how frequently the "public interest" lined up precisely with the private interest of a party seeking special privileges.

You have probably heard this argument: "we should discard economics because it assumes people are rational, and we know from experience that people are anything but." First, this mistakes a modeling convention for a description of our actual mental processes; as the economist David Skarbek put it on Twitter, "Rational Choice Theory is not a theory of cognition." Smith knew this, and he based his analysis on people's actions as he observed them. We seek to make ourselves better off, and I think Smith meant this in a broad sense. There are a lot of ways to think about being "better off."

It is a mistake to think of Smith as an apologist for untrammeled greed. He emphasized the power and importance of self-interest not as a defense of ill-mannered egoism but because of what he observed about social processes like markets and politics. His was a theory of order that would get its most full-throated defense in Hayek's discussion of knowledge-generating conversation and exchange processes that create undersigned and spontaneous order.

The Source of Prosperity, according to Smith, was the Division of Labor. Specialization and division of labor increase our dexterity in our chosen task, saving the time we would otherwise spend switching from task to task, and building up familiarity with a task to the point that it led to labor-saving innovation. The division of labor was limited by the extent of the market. The larger our range of potential collaborators—and I use that word intentionally, as markets are collaborative spaces—the greater our ability to divide labor, specialize, and be more productive.

Smith argued that the *natural* progress of opulence—the title of one of his chapters in the *Wealth of Nations* (*WN*)—was a product of the division of labor and of the liberty we have to buy and sell. This notion of natural progress struck me, and a study of Smith's use of *natural* could yield insight into the fundamental principles of the classical liberal tradition. Here he is in *The Wealth of Nations*:

> "Every individual is continually exerting himself to find out the most advantageous employment for whatever capital he can command. It is his own advantage, indeed, and not that of the society, which he has in view. But the study of his own advantage naturally, or rather necessarily, leads him to prefer that employment which is most advantageous to the society."

When we are free to buy, sell, or build better mousetraps, we get richer. First, we get richer by moving goods from lower-value to higher-value uses. We don't need to create any new material goods. An Alabama fan with an Auburn ticket and an Auburn fan with an Alabama ticket can be better off by swapping. They don't create any new tickets or any new football, but the tickets move from those who don't value them very highly to those who do.

Second, as Smith points out, we prosper because of the division of labor. As Ludwig von Mises and Friedrich Hayek would show in the twentieth century, socialism can't work as a complex division of labor because the absence of markets for the means of production short-circuits the information-generating process that allows us to measure costs accurately. Without prices, we cannot measure the gaps between what gets produced and what people use to produce it. Furthermore, we don't get the information about what it will take to harness and deploy others' knowledge without exchange. As Hayek would show, competition is a *discovery* procedure, and as James Buchanan would later explain, order is defined in the process of its emergence. I believe with Steven Landsburg that the universe is a fundamentally mathematical object, but there is no set of discoverable equations governing social reality the way there is a set of discoverable equations governing physical reality. This is not to say there aren't rules: consider the law of demand and the law of comparative advantage. These, though, are broad insights about general tendencies, not functional forms into which phenomena can be squeezed and thereby manipulated. The social world, like the economy, can be understood. No one can plan it.

Here I wish to reintroduce you to one character and introduce you to a new character in Smith through a few quotes. The Man of System (from *The Theory of Moral Sentiments*) and The Statesman (from *WN*) are pictures of Smith's conviction that trying to control others' lives is the height of presumption and folly. First, The Man of System:

> The man of system ... seems to imagine that he can arrange the different members of a great society with as much ease as the hand arranges the different pieces upon a chess-board. He does not consider that the pieces upon the chess-board have no other principle of motion besides that which the hand impresses upon them; but that, in the great chess-board of human society, every single piece has a principle of motion of its own, altogether different from that which the legislature might choose to impress upon it.

And now The Statesman (forgive me for this very long passage):

The produce of industry is what it adds to the subject or materials upon which it is employed. In proportion as the value of this produce is great or small, so will likewise be the profits of the employer. But it is only for the sake of profit that any man employs a capital in the support of industry; and he will always, therefore, endeavour to employ it in the support of that industry of which the produce is likely to be of the greatest value, or to exchange for the greatest quantity either of money or of other goods. ... But the annual revenue of every society is always precisely equal to the exchangeable value of the whole annual produce of its industry, or rather is precisely the same thing with that exchangeable value. As every individual, therefore, endeavours as much as he can both to employ his capital in the support of domestick industry, and so to direct that industry that its produce may be of the greatest value; every individual necessarily labours to render the annual revenue of the society as great as he can. He generally, indeed, neither intends to promote the publick interest, nor knows how much he is promoting it. By preferring the support of domestick to that of foreign industry, he intends only his own security; and by directing that industry in such a manner as its produce may be of the greatest value, he intends only his own gain, and he is in this, as in many other cases, led by an invisible hand to promote an end which was no part of his intention. Nor is it always the worse for the society that it was no part of it. By pursuing his own interest he frequently promotes that of the society more effectually than when he really intends to promote it. I have never known much good done by those who affected to trade for the publick good. It is an affectation, indeed, not very common among merchants, and very few words need be employed in dissuading them from it. ...

What is the species of domestick industry which his capital can employ, and of which the produce is likely to be of the greatest value, every individual, it is evident, can, in his local situation, judge much better than any statesman or lawgiver can do for him. The statesman, who should attempt to direct private people in what manner they ought to employ their capitals, would not only load himself with a most unnecessary attention, but assume an authority which could safely be trusted, not only to no single person, but to no council or senate whatever, and which would nowhere be so dangerous as in the hands of a man who had folly and presumption enough to fancy himself fit to exercise it.

The Man of System and The Statesman are powerful because of special interests, but that's not all. They are also powerful because of our ideas about social organization. It's true for mundane evils like transportation monopolies and business licensing. It's hard to beat City Hall because a lot of people *believe in* City Hall and conflate "the rule of law" with "the rule of regulators and legislators" (John Cochrane has written an excellent essay on this). It's true, too, for greater evils, some deliberate like segregation and others merely possessing negative unintended consequences, like minimum wages. It's also true for great evils like communism and fascism. These ideologies swept over large parts of the world not over the people's objections but to their thunderous applause.

Recent events show us that *Ideas Have Consequences*, to quote the title of Richard Weaver's classic. The ideas we encounter and process—those that become a part of our being—create the lenses through which we see and interpret events. Who are we? What does it mean to be human? What is a life rightly lived? What does it mean to flourish? These are the kinds of questions you get to ask in the academy. More than this, you get to ask historical and social scientific questions. Under what institutional conditions do individuals and societies flourish? What is *justice*? What, traditionally, has attenuated flourishing, and what if anything can we or should we do for members of historically marginalized groups? How can we get beyond visceral, emotional, or aesthetic reactions and understand what is happening?

Ideas have consequences, literally for better or for worse. Historically, liberty has not been the norm. In just the last century or so, people who should presumably know better have at various times and in various places embraced total war, genocide, eugenics, and gulags. Intellectuals have embraced ideas—nationalism, socialism, and national socialism—that combined with modern technology, created industrial-strength killing machines that almost drowned civilization in blood. This is the legacy we inherit. What legacy will we leave for those who come after us?

During a visit to Samford University, the theologian Stanley Hauerwas pointed out that college students have *four years* to read great books and asked, "Why waste it on not learning how to *read*?" Why indeed? Maybe it seems pointless or impractical, and I'll be the first to admit Smith is difficult. Tolstoy is difficult. We read them despite their difficulty because they make us grapple with ideas that transcend time and space.

In *The Idea of a Christian College*, the philosopher Arthur F. Holmes points to the question we're all asking when tasked with something difficult that doesn't seem very practical: "What am I going to do with this?" He notes that we are asking the wrong question. Instead, we should be asking, "What will these ideas do to me? What kind of person am I becoming because I am encountering these ideas?" In reading Smith, you become a person who better understands our moral sentiments and the nature and causes of the wealth of nations. I don't say that lightly: you gain a more precise understanding of how the world works. You earn, in short, an appreciation for the conditions—embodied in "the obvious and simple system of natural liberty"—that have made us not only more prosperous but also more humane.

When Adam Smith talks about "self-love," he isn't telling people to be self-absorbed. Instead, I think he is making a point about human dignity in the face of cognitive and moral limitations. A lot of economic analysis consists of tracing the implications of exchange and the institutions that make exchange possible. Embedded in exchange, though, is an ethical assumption: you have the right to make an offer, but the person to whom you are making the offer has the right to say "no." An exchange is not a zero-sum game, and you have to work for other people if you want them to work for you.

This isn't, as we might suspect, an apology for the worst forms of selfishness. It's an implicit recognition that other people have wants and rights that count. In *The Wealth of Nations*, Adam Smith explains how we get our dinner by appealing *not* to the "humanity" of the butcher, the brewer, and the baker but by appealing to their "self-love:"

"It is not from the benevolence of the butcher, the brewer, or the baker, that we expect our dinner, but from their regard to their own interest. We address ourselves, not to their humanity but to their self-love, and never talk to them of our own necessities but of their advantages."

It looks like advice to be *selfish* and have faith in the market to work things out. It isn't, though. As Smith notes just before this passage, "man has almost constant occasion for the help of his brethren, and it is vain to expect it from their benevolence only":

> "He will be more likely to prevail if he can interest their self-love in his favour, and show them that it is for their own advantage to do for him what he requires of them. Whoever offers to another a bargain of any kind, proposes to do this. Give me

that which I want, and you shall have this which you want, is the meaning of every such offer; and it is in this manner that we obtain from one another the far greater part of those good offices which we stand in need of."

Smith recognizes our cognitive and moral limitations while also acknowledging genuine disagreement about what is *good*. Consider: I know my friends and my own family pretty well. I probably don't know you or yours that well. When I show up at the butcher shop or the bakery or the bar, I'm not there because I want to take care of the butcher's or baker's or brewer's family and friends. I want to take care of my own. To enlist the butcher, the baker, and the brewer in this endeavor, I have to persuade them that they would help themselves and those they care about by helping me. I have to convince them that helping me is the best use of their time and energy compared to the alternatives. Even entirely altruistic, utterly non-selfish butchers, bakers, and brewers will have to make these determinations. Even if I am unselfish, I have to make these determinations, as well. "Self-interest" and "self-love" need not be hedonistic or self-absorbed in the ways we try to convince our children not to be. Voluntary exchange recognizes different interests, goals, values, and beliefs, and it is an efficient, dignity-respecting, and dare I say dignity-*enhancing* way for people to cooperate.

In his 2002 book *A Theory of the State*, the economist Yoram Barzel writes that *exchange* is the mechanism that allows us to enjoy the benefits of specialization. In the "Statesman" passage above, Smith makes one of his most misunderstood claims. The invisible hand of the marketplace converts our self-interest into the public interest. We *intend* to make the world a better place according to our preferences. Others' ability to make the world a better place according to their preferences is the *unintended* consequence. By maximizing their own wellbeing, "every individual necessarily labours to render the annual revenue of the society as great as we can."

Smith observes a pattern and an outcome. An investor, entrepreneur, or manager directs his (in the eighteenth century, it was almost always "his") time, talent, and treasure toward the most profitable industries. To the extent that he supports "domestic industry," it is not because he wishes to do so *per se* but because this is most conducive to "his own security" as measured by his desire for profit and risk tolerance.

He encounters four problems, though. First, his wants are unlimited. No matter how much he has, he can almost certainly think of ways he could use even more. These uses needn't be "selfish." I enjoy traveling, and I plan to do more of it as my income increases. I can also think of many ways I can support spiritual, humanitarian, and intellectual causes I support. Second, resources are scarce. If Adam eats the whole apple, Eve can't have any. The baker cannot knead the dough and chop firewood in the same instant. That blob of plastic can become a coffee stirrer or a guitar pick, but not both at the same time. Material resources are scarce.

Third, he doesn't share others' talents, tastes, and values. Should the land grow apples in the first place, or should it grow oranges? Should the baker knead dough or chop firewood? Guitar players and coffee drinkers might have very different views about whether this specific piece of plastic should become a guitar pick or a coffee stirrer. I'm not saying there should be *only* guitar picks or *only* coffee stirrers. A given piece of plastic of a given type, composition, and quality can only become one or the other.

Fourth, he doesn't share others' knowledge. I know little about chemical engineering and plastics. I wouldn't know where to begin to make a coffee stirrer or a guitar pick. Maybe "buy some plastic," but I don't know what kind of plastic is best for coffee stirrers and what type is best for guitar picks. There are people in the world who know—and some of them are probably reading this article—but I don't.

Enter the invisible hand of the market. Exchange reveals the patterns of specialization, division of labor, and production that are most consistent with consumers' preferences. Others' talents, tastes, values, and knowledge constitute the invisible hand. I convey information about my skills, tastes, values, and knowledge with offers to buy or sell. Others convey their understanding of the degree to which their skills, tastes, values, and knowledge are compatible with mine by their willingness to accept my bids and offers. I am led by the invisible hand of prices that reflect others' knowledge.

Here's an example. Consider a 100 calorie pack of almonds.[5] How did the invisible hand work here? I bought the almonds at Target, accepting their offer of seven 100 calorie packs of almonds for something like $3.50 and rejecting their offers of everything else I could have bought with that $3.50. Target made an arrangement with Emerald to stock those specific almonds on that specific part of that specific shelf at that specific time of that specific day anticipating that *someone*—they need not know who or why—would be willing to accept the trade. Emerald agreed to sell the almonds to (or through, depending on their contractual arrangements) Target because they expected Target to sell them most quickly at an attractive price. They produced almonds instead of anything else they could have done with those resources because they expected profits.

And so on, throughout every successful and failed exchange that went into the production of some almonds. Others' knowledge about their talents, tastes, values, and preferences guides me to offer $3.50 for the almonds. At a lower price, the people who made the almonds might have done something else. At a higher price, I might have bought peanuts instead of almonds. Prices encode our relevant knowledge. The invisible hand leads us toward exchanges that make people better off and away from exchanges that make people worse off.

As the economist Paul Heyne put it in his book *Are Economists Basically Immoral?*, market exchange means "everyone wins, or at least everyone with the right to be consulted" (p. 3). The parties to the transaction are the ones who have skin in the game, and they are the only ones who have the right to be consulted.

Observers might disapprove of the transaction for a lot of reasons. I may be making a grievous mistake: the back of the almond packet says, "Partially Produced with Genetic Engineering." Maybe the "Partially Produced with Genetic Engineering" almonds are turning my internal stomach and intestines into tumors as I write this. I'm nearly certain they're not. The only reason I don't write "completely certain" is that I will acknowledge some probability close to but slightly greater than zero that almonds "Partially Produced with Genetic Engineering" are pure cancer fuel or the stuff of supervillain origin stories. The probability that genetic engineering harms me is probably a lot lower than the damage from eschewing almonds for something less healthy.

Observers might disapprove. What happens if they swap the visible fist of the state for the invisible hand of the market? In doing so, they destroy potentially valuable knowledge about the risks I will take. Furthermore, the state allows observers to substitute their reasoning without paying a meaningful price beyond merely having an opinion about something. It's easy to conjure up a vivid nightmare scenario in which I am breathing my last in a hospital room, the air heavy with my regret at having eaten the wrong almonds. I don't have any trouble conjuring up a nightmare scenario in which this happens to one of my children. Swapping the state's visible fist for the market's invisible hand says that some knowledge has no place in the conversation.

## 10

# Beer or Grape-Nuts?

I got to tour the Samuel Adams Brewery in Boston in 2019. It was a fantastic tour of a surprisingly small facility—it reminded me less of the Budweiser brewery tour from my graduate school days in St. Louis and more of the Schlafly brewery tour from…my graduate school days in St. Louis. Producing even a simple and ancient good (like beer) in a modern economy is mind-blowingly complex.

I know very little about beer. I know it was historically significant, and I know that it gets its alcoholic content from yeast eating sugar and pooping out alcohol. I may not even be describing that correctly. The more I study economics and liberal political economy, the more I'm impressed with the importance of decentralized knowledge—specifically, knowledge of "the particular circumstances of time and place"—and the feedback markets provide. Here are a few comments on some things I learned.

---

Carden, Art. 2019. "Barley and Beer: The Sam Adams Story." American Institute for Economic Research. July 22.

First, there are only *two* types of beer: lager and ale. I didn't know that and don't remember which yeasts do what, so I won't try to recall. Every beer product out there comes from one of only two different kinds of yeast. It's quite a variety within two categories.

Second, hops absorb what's in the soil in which it grows, so the broad category of "hops" has many manifestations. They don't use hops from Boston, the tour guide said, because it tastes like student loan debt. Haha. They have to be very particular about their hops—which come from Germany—to maintain uniform quality. Note who is in charge here. In a competitive market, the consumer calls the tune. In this case, the message the brewers are getting is "be very particular about the hops you use."

Third, the original Samuel Adams beers used Boston tap water—but Samuel Adams also has breweries in Cincinnati and Pennsylvania's Lehigh Valley. To maintain consistency, they send samples from Boston to the Cincinnati and Lehigh Valley breweries and then modify the water in those locations to match the Boston water as closely as they can get it. At first glance, it seems like water is water, but to maintain uniform quality, Samuel Adams has taken what looks like a pretty extreme step—but it is a step that, in their estimation, their customers demand.

Most interestingly, I learned during the beginning of the tour that they roast barley to different grades for different beers *and* that barley is *also* the main ingredient in Grape-Nuts. Here's a fine example of the problem markets solve that states really can't. Should we use barley to make beer, or should we use it to make Grape-Nuts? How will we know we have succeeded in a world where we don't know one another's preferences or dispositions? The market test of profit-and-loss provides people with reliable feedback. If the financial return to the barley used to make beer is higher than the financial return to the barley used to make Grape-Nuts, beer wins. If the return to the barley used to make

Grape-Nuts is higher than the financial return to the barley used to make beer, then Grape-Nuts wins.

The profit motive drives us to the "right" allocation of barley between Grape-Nuts and different beers. If Grape-Nuts are inordinately profitable, Grape-Nut production will expand, and beer production will contract. If there are big profits in beer, beer production will grow while Grape-Nut production shrinks. The process stops when the return on the marginal grain of barley is the same in either use. In the real world, of course, there are all sorts of complicating factors—regulatory barriers to entry are one example—that slow the process, but this is part of the essential logic of competition. The profit motive drives people to get resources into the hands of those who will make the best use of them, where "best" concerns people's willingness to pay with the dollars they earn by the sweat of their brow. We may disapprove of people's choices and think they should eat more Grape-Nuts and drink less beer, but I'm not prepared to privilege the beliefs of mere observers who pay no meaningful price for being wrong over the revealed preferences of the people with the strongest incentives to choose wisely.

A government could, undoubtedly, make *beer*. But the *right* beer with the *right* flavor profiles for a world of nearly-infinite variety of tastes—not all of them consistent? For that, you need a market.

# 11

# You Want *How Much* for an Undershirt?

"What do you need?"

"Undershirts." I was in a hotel gift shop and not optimistic.

"Right this way."

I was surprised. *I guess the shop has undershirts, after all*, I thought. I had my usual rhapsodic feelings about how people who don't necessarily care about me are nonetheless able to care for me by having shirts when and where I might need them. I have, after all, bought belts, sunglasses, shoes, suits, shirts, and all sorts of other things on the road when I've opened my suitcase and discovered (to my horror) that I've forgotten something.

Then I looked at the price and thought again about just how badly I needed shirts. Another shirt would've been nice to have, but not at that price.

My natural impulse was to feel frustrated and maybe even a little offended. After all, I was but a weary traveler who wanted an undershirt.

---

Carden, Art. 2019. "Why that Hotel Shop Undershirt Is So Expensive." American Institute for Economic Research. November 27.

I thought the people at the little shop were there for me, but actually, they were trying to exploit me in my time of need.

Then I overcame my first wave of emotion and started thinking about it more carefully. Did I *need* a shirt? Or did I just *want* a shirt? I was flying home early the next morning, so I could've made do with what was in my suitcase. Perhaps I wouldn't have been as comfortable, but I would've been okay (update: I was OK).

The price played an indispensable role in my undershirt mini-adventure. The people who owned the shop had undershirts, dress shirts, socks, underwear, ties, belts, and everything else that people like me are prone to forget. The price was crucial to an exercise in economic triage: it forced me to ask whether I wanted the shirts now or if I would be willing to wait for perhaps a better price somewhere else and leave the shirts for someone who might want them even more dearly than I did.

At first glance, it might seem inefficient for the shirts to be on the rack instead of on someone's back. Just because no one is wearing the shirts doesn't mean people waste them. As W.H. Hutt (1977) might argue, the shirts specialize in availability, with the price telling people to think hard about whether they *need* shirts right now or whether they could do without, at least for the short term. The shirts stop specializing in availability when someone in a bind finds himself in need of men's undershirts at a hotel in Fort Lauderdale, Florida, on short notice.

A price might look like an arbitrary imposition, a needless barrier between me and what I need. "Need," however, is pretty malleable, and people are pretty creative. As Julian Simon argued, people come up with all sorts of ingenious ways to solve the problems they face. It can be something as mundane as deciding to go without a new undershirt for a few hours or something as complex as reimagining an entire production-and-operations process in response to higher prices of fuel and raw materials.

## You Want *How Much* for an Undershirt?

The "sharing economy" is an example, and here I borrow from Michael Munger's *Tomorrow 3.0*. Transaction costs—which are the costs of finding people with whom to trade (triangulation), processing payments (transfer), and verifying the integrity of what is exchanged (trust)—have, until relatively recently, eaten the world. There was probably someone at the hotel with a shirt that would have fit me who might have been willing to lend or rent me a shirt. We don't bother with that now because the cost of arranging the exchange is simply too high.

"They're still cheaper at Walmart and Target. You're getting ripped off." Maybe. God bless them; Walmart and Target have bailed out this absentminded professor more times than I care to admit. The people running the shop know more about what F. A. Hayek called "the particular circumstances of time and place," however. Shirts at Walmart and Target are cheap because they sell in such high volume in stores sitting on acres of cheap suburban land.

By contrast, the little shop at the hotel is on an expensive beachfront where shelf space is a lot more valuable. Think about all the things that could be on the shelves other than shirts. Knickknacks. Breath mints. Candy. Aspirin. Bodice-ripper novels. I imagine all are hot sellers at a beachfront hotel, but the people calling the shots are the ones with the sales data I don't have.

Compared to a lot of the alternatives, plain white t-shirts are bulky and low value. They probably don't sell as briskly as a lot of other things. Having your money tied up in inventory is expensive—it could be earning interest, after all—and the shopkeepers aren't going to keep the shirts on hand unless they're compensated for this, too. It's only worth the store's while to stock the shirts if they have a pretty good idea that they'll have a steady-enough stream of conventioneers, wedding guests, and others who want t-shirts (or ties, or socks, or underwear, or dress shirts) in a pinch. Otherwise, they could (and would) stock other stuff.

As Adam Smith explained so long ago, commerce is persuasion. I paraphrase: every bid and every ask in a free market is an act of oratory with one saying to another, "Give me that which I want, and I will give you this which you want." At the beachfront hotel shop, that's what the shopkeepers were saying by putting a pack of undershirts on the shelf and asking what they did. In this case, I said, "No, thank you"—and I left the shirts there for someone who wants them more than me.

## 12

# How Do You Get to the Studio? Ask a Stranger

The phone rang. Someone from a Chinese television station asked me to be on their show "The Link" the next day to talk about the new Costco in Shanghai. I agreed, they booked me a spot at a studio downtown, and we confirmed everything via email. Class ended at 9:05, and I told them I would be at the studio by 9:45 for a 10:00 AM broadcast. Not a problem.

The morning of the broadcast, I was driving to work when I thought through the logistics again. Parking on campus is always a nightmare for the first few days of a new semester, and we were on day 3. I'd had to hustle to make it to my 1 PM on day one because parking was pretty chaotic. Having arrived early, I hesitated to give up the prime parking spot I had secured and burden myself with the task of finding on-campus parking again and then remembering where I had parked.

That's not all. Generally, Birmingham is a pretty easy place to get around; however, many construction projects were going on the day of

---

Carden, Art. 2019. "How Do You Get to Carnegie Hall?" American Institute for Economic Research. August 29.

the show. That means closed streets, and finding parking in any major city can be an adventure of its own. I also couldn't recall what it would cost me to park in one of the decks near the studio's location at the Birmingham-Jefferson Convention Complex.

There's an alternative, though: I could call a cab or use a ride-sharing service like Uber or Lyft. To have someone drive me would cost about $30-$35 for a round trip. As luck would have it, it was our first day of really exploring the Big Ideas in Economics, and I thought it might be useful to bring them to bear on this knotty issue. Therefore, I decided to ask my students: how should I get to the studio? Should I drive myself? Or should I take an Uber?

At first glance, it seems obvious: drive yourself. According to Apple Maps, it's about a fifteen-minute drive. By driving myself, I wouldn't have to shell out for someone to get me there and back. There are a lot of hidden costs that are easy to overlook, though. There's the gas I'd burn. It would probably be about a gallon going round trip to downtown. There's what I might have to pay for parking. There's the stress that comes with driving (which I hate), which could deplete the precious reserves of willpower that might keep me from making terrible choices about what I ate at lunch. There's the depreciation on my car. There's the fact that I can rip through my email and other bits of correspondence if I have someone else doing the driving for me. There's also the possibility of causing an accident, as I probably would have been marginally more distracted than my Uber driver. There are costs, and there are benefits, and if we are going to choose wisely, we need to be very clear about what *all* of the costs and benefits are—or at least the costs and benefits that were worth acknowledging.

The students voted. By a slim majority, they chose Uber.

Navigating construction-carved downtown Birmingham was, as I expected, a bit of an adventure. Still, my driver was able to pick me up at the door of Cooney Hall on Samford's campus and drop me off exactly where I needed to be. Then, on my way home, I was able to have an Uber driver pick me up near the door and then again drop me off exactly where I needed to be. I could process email, do a few other tasks while en route in both directions, and avoid the stress that might have made me capitulate when I passed a plate of delectable-looking brownies at the cafeteria.

It was the right choice in that context. It's not the right choice in every context, though. I asked my afternoon class about whether I should pick up my kids from karate myself or send Uber to get them. My afternoon students voted overwhelmingly in favor of me going and picking up the kids myself. I'm not sure Uber would have picked them up, and I'm not sure their karate teacher would let them in the car with a seemingly-random person who says, "I'm their Uber driver." It's also on my way home, and as one student pointed out, having Uber pick them up would cut into the time I get to spend with them.

To be honest, asking whether or not I should tell Uber to pick up and deliver my kids this evening was kind of absurd. It was an exercise in applying some of the big ideas we had considered so far, like incentives, trade-offs, and thinking at the margin. Importantly, my brief interactions with Uber that morning show how markets help us care *for* one another without necessarily caring that much *about* one another. I certainly don't wish any ill on the drivers, but I don't care about them in the same way I care about my children. They don't care about me in the same way they care about their loved ones.

A technology-enlarged market made it a lot easier for us to cooperate. I cared for the loved ones of my drivers and the people who work for Uber by paying them for a ride, giving them something they no doubt find useful. The strangers at Uber cared for *my* loved ones by making it easier for me to get to and from the studio safely—and markets made it possible for them to do it without explicitly intending it.

## 13

# Innovate to Help Strangers During Pandemics

During periods of great uncertainty, it is customary to hear calls for someone "with a plan." The COVID-19 pandemic has, of course, been no different in this response. Politicians, commentators, and frightened members of the public are looking—with misplaced faith, I believe—toward places like Washington, DC, the state capital, or the mayor's office for someone with a clear, articulated solution that will put all this behind us.

The air is thick with what-ifs, and the Internet is thick with memes mocking long-haired freaks who want to end the lockdowns and get haircuts, or on the opposite side of the transaction, so they can cut hair. *What*, people wonder, is *The Plan*? We get nervous when it becomes clear that there simply isn't one. Some of us chalk it up to incompetence or malice and then go looking for someone "who can make a plan work."

---

Carden, Art. 2020. "We Don't Need One Big Plan to End the Lockdown." American Institute for Economic Research. May 15.

We can do better. The problem isn't identifying and implementing One Plan to Rule Them All. The problem, such as it is, is to coordinate and integrate the disparate and often-conflicting plans of the almost eight billion people on the planet. Just as no single mind (or central committee of minds) knows how to make a pencil, no single mind (or central committee of minds) knows how to plan an epidemic response. It's easy to speak in terms of very vague generalities like "food" and "medicine" and "shelter" and "education," but once we get into the details, it's hard to go much beyond that. I'll use myself and my family as an illustration and show how no one knows how to plan a society-wide Covid-19 response.

"Solutions" aren't created and imposed by our cognitive betters. They bubble up, often in undesigned and unarticulated patterns. Software and information technology illustrate. Suddenly, many people had to move their operations online, and demand for online meeting solutions rose. Many got into computer science and computer engineering out of sheer fascination or a desire to make the world a better place. Some people get into it for the money. Some are left-wing revolutionaries. Importantly, I don't have to know or approve of people's motives to cooperate with them and use their knowledge to advance my ends. They don't have to know my motives to serve me or use my talents.

We homeschooled before we started sending our kids to a nearby independent, Charlotte Mason-influenced school, so we were able to make a smoother transition than some from our routine to schooling at home. It meant making some adjustments, and I turned our front porch into my new "office."

When my classes moved online, I needed to expand my technological capabilities. I bought a pair of Apple AirPod Pro noise-canceling headphones. A few years ago, I got life-changing Bose QC-35s, which I proceeded to lose on a trip in October 2017. The AirPods have been incredible. They fit my ears very comfortably. They almost entirely cancel out a lot of the low rumble of urban noise (air conditioners, far-off street noise) and seriously muffle other noise (nearby street noise, lawnmowers). I can still hear most birdsong (not a bad thing), but for the most part, I'm able to enjoy remarkable quiet amid urban (and domestic) chaos.

Do I know how they work? Not without googling it, and even then, I know sufficiently little about sound engineering and physics to *understand* what is going on. I'll take Apple's word for it; in my experience with their customer service personnel, they have been pretty trustworthy (any company with a trillion-dollar-plus valuation has a lot riding on a good customer experience).

Consider the number of people who helped bring me something as simple as a set of noise-canceling headphones. First, there are the engineers. They designed the product and set it up to meet my "demanding" specifications. As with a pencil, I can harness and deploy knowledge I don't have for purposes the engineers may not understand. It goes deeper than this, though. Someone did the fundamental research to understand sound physics and make a product like noise-canceling wireless earbuds possible.

I haven't scratched the surface of the knowledge I can use in response to the coronavirus pandemic. I dictated an earlier version of this chapter into a Google Document. I can use software programs I didn't write and almost certainly couldn't write to simply speak and have my words transcribed into written text in a Google Document with an impressively low error rate.

Remote technologies have also made social distancing a lot easier. In the 1990s, when I was in college, movie courses online would have almost certainly been far more difficult. The internet as we know it was in its infancy, email was still a relatively new technology, and when I needed to do homework, I had to write with a pen or pencil on paper.

Moving things online has also been made a lot easier by video sharing sites like YouTube and Vimeo. In his 2008 book *Create Your Own Economy*, Tyler Cowen pointed out how a lot of the job of a professor or teacher would increasingly become curation of content. Statista reports that in 2007, people were uploading 6 hours of video to YouTube every minute. By May of 2019, they were uploading about 500 hours of video to YouTube every minute. If your full-time job were to watch YouTube content 40 hours a week, 50 weeks a year, it would take you an entire year working full-time to view about four minutes' worth of uploaded content. Of course, a lot of this is garbage, and a lot of it won't advance our pedagogical goals ("watch these three hours of people playing Minecraft and yelling" doesn't seem like much of a lesson plan). A lot of it, however, is absolute gold.

Finally, to use just one more example, financial services firms are processing payments quickly. I bought my new headphones on Amazon. The money was charged to my credit card and paid to Apple, with Amazon taking their cut. The bill will be paid automatically out of my checking account when it's due. It will happen without much of my attention. I don't have to understand what is working, which electrons are jumping where, or anything about anyone else involved.

Consider the things we use daily that have puzzled previous generations. The iPad is one of my favorite examples. When Apple released it, people mocked the name—I'll admit, I had some sport with it, as well—and a lot of other people saying, "What is it *for*? What is the *point*?" In asking "what's the point," they miss it: what the iPad is *for* is something we discovered over time. The platform's tablets and smartphones make it a lot easier to live, work, learn, and play under a pandemic lockdown.

Commentators with Thomas Sowell's "unconstrained vision" see social problems like the pandemic lockdown as baking bread, just more cognitively demanding. You just need to find the right recipe, the right ingredients, and the right cook: a Great Mind (or committee of great minds). While a lot of us have enjoyed a lot of homemade bread during the COVID-19 pandemic, the recovery problem is of a fundamentally different kind. It involves the coordination of the disparate and often-incompatible plans of billions of minds—and if we wish for that coordination to make the best use of knowledge in society, we are making a mistake if we are looking for a plan.

# 14

# How Much For that Doggy at the Sushi Bar?

People have all kinds of different preferences and like all kinds of different things. We also do all sorts of dumb stuff. Sometimes, we want to share our passion with others, and sometimes we want to keep people from following in our unwise footsteps. By all means, we should work to persuade, but we don't do anyone any favors when we resort to force.

Sometimes, this stems from a simple mistake, where we leap our preferences to others' obligations. "I wouldn't do that job," is fine. "I wouldn't do that job; therefore, *no one* should be allowed to" is not. "I think this subject is important," is fine. "I think this subject is important; therefore, we should require everyone to study it" is not. More generally, "I like doing this thing" is OK. "I like doing this thing; therefore, we should require it of everyone" generally isn't.

---

Carden, Art. 2019. "There Is No One Answer to Rule Them All." American Institute for Economic Research. July 12.

We aren't respecting others' liberty, dignity, and autonomy as independent and independently valuable moral agents when we coerce them. We're also silencing the economic conversation about what people should produce, when, where, how, and for whom. We silence the cultural conversation about what it means to live well by saying some things are out of bounds when there isn't a compelling case that those things affect others enough that maybe—*maybe*—compulsion might be warranted. Many things people want to ban or require don't even get close to a decent case for compulsion.

Consider low-wage jobs in dangerous conditions. It's not something I choose because I have much better options. Who am I to tell someone else to eschew a position I would find unpleasant or accept a wage I wouldn't like, especially if it's the best of a lot of bad options? If we respect people's liberty, dignity, and autonomy and care about their prosperity, we will work to expand their choices rather than limit them.

Or consider studying economics. I've dedicated my life to it, and in my weaker moments, I think no one should be allowed out of college without at least two courses in economics and two courses in statistics. I want to indulge that little voice inside me saying, "There oughta be a law." I have to recognize that not everyone agrees with me. Some people (for reasons I don't understand) think there are some things more important or exciting than economics and statistics. I'd be assuming against the evidence that compelling someone to study something is the same thing as their learning it. The waters muddy quite a bit when we talk about college curricula as colleges and universities are free to set their requirements. Still, each institution, in my opinion, should be free to decide what counts as a degree from that institution.

What about the children? Kids, too, are a little bit different, but we try (not always successfully) to help our kids learn to make good choices by giving them the freedom to make a lot of low-stakes bad ones. My wife and I think we do a decent-enough job. We step in and enforce rules about things like iPads and candy, but there's a clear difference between the appropriate relationship between parents and children and the proper relationship between adult strangers.

Here's a practical example one of my friends shared on social media: pets on porches at Alabama restaurants.[6] According to Alabama's health code, "Live animals may not be allowed on the premises of a food establishment." The rule also means porches, which means pet-friendly Alabama restaurants are out of luck.

The example illustrates why economic liberty matters. Some restaurants want to cater to pet owners. Others are wary of possible complaints from other patrons who don't want to eat in a restaurant with dogs, cats, and the health problems they might create. Other people probably don't care and want to go where the food is good. What one customer likes might be an unbearable imposition upon another.

There is, therefore, no One Answer to Rule Them All. We have a lot of different cuisines to choose from because people have different preferences. Similarly, retailers range from Walmart to boutique cheese shops because people have different preferences about price, selection, knowledgeable staff, and in-store amenities. Who is "right"? Everyone, and no one. The right retail pattern emerges from a dizzying array of bids, offers, and ventures. I don't know what the equilibrium is or should be. Maybe dispensing with pet prohibitions will lead to a profusion of pooches on patios and porches. Or maybe not. And if you don't like one restaurant's policy, odds are there will be another one with an approach that's much more your speed.

## 15

# You Need to Pay Your Employees With The Right Combination of Money and Drugs

A startling realization hit me after a sip of coffee during class the other day. I had just told students a maybe-apocryphal and likely-misremembered story about a pizza delivery driver whose employer paid with cash wages and drugs (tranquilizers and marijuana, if I recall correctly). I laughed at the absurdity of paying employees with drugs when I realized I was drinking coffee—a vehicle for caffeine. Caffeine is my drug of choice, and I had gotten the coffee from the office kitchen.

It's true: *my employer literally pays me in money and drugs.*

They pay me in many other things, for that matter, as people don't work for wages alone. I certainly don't. We supply labor in exchange for a whole host of things in addition to wages: health coverage, life insurance, complimentary coffee in the office kitchen, job satisfaction, job

---

Carden, Art. 2020. What's the Right Mix of Money and Drugs for Your Employees? American Institute for Economic Research September 17.

security, scheduling flexibility, retirement contributions, enjoyment, the sense that we're making a difference, and so on.

I started thinking about the importance of markets in deciding who does what and for how much. It got me thinking about how what we mean by "labor" is "defined in the process of its emergence," to borrow a phrase from James M. Buchanan. It also got me thinking about the consequences of messing with the whole process.

Holding everything else constant, economists argue, fun jobs tend to pay less. People are willing to supply a bit more labor in fun jobs at a given wage than boring jobs. Imagine you could earn $50,000 per year doing something you hate or $50,000 per year doing something you love. Unless you're just a masochist, you will take $50,000 doing something you love (and if you *are* a masochist, then do you *really* hate the non-fun job?). Someone who wishes to lure you into a non-fun position will have to offer additional compensation—like higher wages—to make up for the monotony.

Here's an example. We professors spend a lot of time feeling sorry for ourselves because we don't earn as much as similarly-educated professionals in other fields. We often make *less* than people with even *less* education. As I've heard it said, when you go to graduate school in anticipation of an academic career, you are giving up your current income so you can give up future income.

Our woes ignore how much of our compensation comes in freedom, flexibility, and job satisfaction. We spend a fair amount of time writing reports to satisfy various accreditors, but the paperwork burden isn't *that* high. By and large, people pay us to think, read, write, and talk about things we find fascinating. We call "work" what most people call "leisure." The money is decent, too: a professorial salary is comfortably middle- to upper-middle-class.

In occupations like ours, it isn't clear where work leaves off, and leisure picks up. I recently finished reading Randall Holcombe's 2018 book *Political Capitalism*, most of which I read outside the regular business day. What's more, I enjoyed it, so you could argue that it was *leisure*. At the same time, I'm going to use it in my teaching, research, and writing, so you could also argue that it was *labor*. The Man of System who imagines he can arrange the members of a great society with the same ease with which he arranges the pieces on a chessboard is not well-positioned to make this judgment. I am—for myself, anyway. I can think about what I might do in your situation, but since I don't actually enjoy the benefits or realize the costs of the choices you're considering, my advice might not be worth that much. I'm certainly not in any position to compel you to act against your will.

"Hold on," you might say. "many low-paying jobs are hazardous, and many high-paying jobs aren't. You don't face many occupational hazards sitting at a desk in the offices of a New York law firm or a Birmingham university." That's true, but it doesn't mean the economic analysis is wrong. The critical phrase in thinking about the laws of demand and supply is *all else held constant*. People with low productivity and bad options will not have as much ability to choose combinations of wages and working conditions. People with high productivity and good options, on the other hand, can be pickier. Empirically, people tend to be willing to accept a lot of risk in exchange for slightly higher wages far lower on the productivity distribution. As people get more productive and as their options improve, they tend to be willing to sacrifice wages for workplace comfort. It's hardly clear that we can make them better off by presuming to make their choices for them.

Altogether, this is one of the reasons why market processes matter. I can sit in my office, staring at my navel, and think about a bunch of "nice if" scenarios or dream up a bunch of things to which I think people have a right. However, I lack knowledge of "the particular circumstances of time and place." Contexts differ in ways that might not be apparent to me as an ivory tower observer. Some people will want to work for a company that expresses their most deeply-held values. Some people will value the thrill and fulfillment that comes with being a risk-taking entrepreneur. Others will prefer job security. Others will be willing to accept lower job security for higher wages. Others might appreciate an excellent dental plan. Some people want drugs (like coffee). A central authority cannot plan a "right" combination of wages, benefits, and other perquisites. It emerges from trial and error in the market.

## 16

# The Market Loves You— and Your Little Dog, Too.

After a bit of cajoling, my wife and I capitulated and allowed our kids to get a dog. Lucy, a black lab mix, is the newest addition to our family and follows in the footsteps of JoJo, the adorable white bunny we got at the end of summer 2019.

Naturally, there were all sorts of things we needed to get started. My wife went to the pet shop to get dishes, a leash, food, and all the other stuff you need. When she got home, I helped her unload the new chew toys, the food and water dishes, the massive bag of dog food, and so on. All the while, I kept saying to myself, *don't look at the receipt, don't look at the receipt, don't look at the receipt…*

I looked at the receipt. Then I had a moment of silence for our checking account.

Then something became very real to me. Capitalism, as Deirdre McCloskey defines it, is a system in which people voluntarily trade

---

Carden, Art. 2020. "The Market Loves You–And Your Little Dog, Too." American Institute for Economic Research. June 13.

private property and free labor, governed by the rule of law and an ethical consensus—means our *dog* will have a higher standard of living than our ancestors did—and, tragically, a higher standard of living than a lot of people in the world right now.

Part of what makes this so interesting to me is that there is a lot more play in pet adoption than narrow self-interest and the profit motive. We adopted Lucy from a local nonprofit organization that provides foster homes for unwanted animals and then tries to give them permanent homes. They are very clearly concerned with pet welfare very broadly, as they make sure that every animal in that place has been fixed, vaccinated, and microchipped. She is also housebroken. I remembered what Bob Barker said at the end of every episode of "The Price is Right" when I was growing up: have your pets spayed or neutered, and help control the population.

They encourage responsible pet ownership. The foster caretaker we dealt with gave us several recommendations for pet food, appropriate toys, and proper play. Interestingly, she mentioned that she does not buy anything made in China because there are less stringent regulations. She noted that in several cases, animals have gotten sick from products made in China. While she does not trust products made in China, she does trust products made by Purina. For example, she noted that they do a lot of testing with dogs like Lucy in mind. Of course, she said that dog food from Kirkland is fine. These are voluntary trades of private property, but not, in this case, guided by the profit motive.

What would motivate Purina? Why wouldn't they cut corners to make a quick buck? People feel very strongly about family pets, and making lousy products that second them might not be a good long-run strategy. Our kids are beside themselves with joy because we have a new pet, and the fact that we have and can care for a pet is the result of the efforts of armies of people we will probably never meet who may not even care about dogs or rabbits. However, their attention to their families, their goals, their desires, and their values have induced them to help us.

As of this writing, hundreds of millions of human beings live on less than $1.25 a day. That's $1.25 worth of food, clothing, and shelter every single day. It isn't unlike the living standards our ancestors "enjoyed" pretty much since humans started walking upright. And yet, it pales in comparison to the food, clothing, shelter, and entertainment our dog gets to enjoy. Did it happen because of the government? Redistribution? Welfare? Not mainly. It happened because of enormous increases in our ability to produce food, clothing, and shelter—increases so enormous that we can feed amply, "clothe" (with a collar), and shelter a big dog we got just for the joy of having her around.

I spend a lot of time and energy thinking about how free people in free markets raise living standards and how they make my children materially better off. After looking at the receipt from the pet supply store, it became evident to me that free people in free markets are making it so that our animal friends are mind-blowingly better off, as well.

In 2019, my former AIER colleague Jeffrey Tucker published a collection of essays titled *The Market Loves You*. It seems pretty clear from our experience getting a dog that the market doesn't just love us—it loves our dog, too.

# PART III

# Good Names and Great Riches: How Strangers Help You Avoid Getting Ripped Off

# 17

# Can the Market Protect You From a Bad Haircut?

In 2019, Arkansas will have a golden opportunity to make life better and more affordable for regular Arkansans. KATV Little Rock reported on legislation that would abolish the Arkansas Barber Board.[7] According to KATV, "Under the bill, barbers would register with the Department of Health, paying a $50 registration fee as well as a $2,000 surety bond. Licensed cosmetologists would not be required to file a registration or bond if the cosmetologist practices barbering as part of its services."

Removing licensing restrictions would be a big step toward a freer labor market and more opportunities for people looking for ways to put food on their tables and clothes on their backs. I think it's a no-brainer.

Not everyone agrees, of course. The new rules must overcome the special pleading of special-privilege-seeking special interests. And that's a formidable roadblock.

---

Carden, Art. 2019. "Abolish the Barber Board." American Institute for Economic Research. March 13.

As one might expect, barbers and the operators of barber schools are unhappy about it. Barbers descended on Little Rock to voice their displeasure.[8] They are upset about the end of "professionalism" that comes from the end of the barbering board, and there are, of course, health concerns. A business that involves fluids, sharp blades, and near-constant contact with skin and hair runs the risk of transmitting fungus and diseases. Quality is an understandable concern.

But notably, eliminating state requirements doesn't mean *prohibiting* people from differentiating themselves with quality certification. Barbering schools are also understandably upset about eliminating the regulations because doing so might cut directly into their business. However, there are a lot of creative ways to adapt to a brave new world of unlicensed Arkansas barbering. Barbers will need to differentiate themselves based on quality and not permission.

But what about the hapless consumer? Think it possible that the consumer isn't so hapless—especially in a world where there are online rating systems for everything. Some people might accept risks or trade quality for lower prices, but barbers can adapt. I'm reminded of a joke that illustrates this: A barber was worried when a shop opened across the street advertising $6 haircuts. After a flash of inspiration, he posted a sign saying, "We Fix $6 Haircuts." Brand names like Sport Clips, Supercuts, and SmartStyle convey a lot of important information about quality and cleanliness. I suspect that for quality and "professionalism" in the market for haircuts, things like Yelp reviews are more effective than licensing.

Think about fast food. Chick-fil-A is almost always so clean that you could probably eat off the floor. They don't do this because the health department is looking over their shoulders. Some restaurants pass inspection where it's not clear you're safe to eat off the table. Chick-fil-A can charge premium prices and maintain considerable brand loyalty by providing a consistently excellent product. They do this because it's profitable.

Not every restaurant is as reliably clean as Chick-fil-A, but those restaurants offer different value propositions. Maybe they offer lower prices, a bigger selection, or one-on-every-street-corner convenience. None of these are self-evidently "right," and none are self-evidently "wrong." Consumers vote for "right" and "wrong" ways to run restaurants or barbershops with their every purchase. In a free market, there is room to at least try practically any crazy business model—and there's room for a lot of them to stick around.

Let's make this numerical. Suppose the 3,000,000 or so Arkansans each get their hair cut every five or six weeks. Nine haircuts per Arkansan is 27,000,000 haircuts per year. Now suppose eliminating the regulation reduces the average price of a haircut by $1. That reduces barbers' incomes by $27,000,000 in total. That might seem like a terrible thing until we realize that the $27,000,000 barbers lose ends up in consumers' pockets. Take note of the law of demand: as haircut prices fall, people get more haircuts. The benefit to consumers, $27,000,000 plus whatever net benefit they get from extra haircuts, is larger than the barbers' losses from eliminating the regulations. Arkansans are better off because it's easier to become a barber. (N.B.: Steven Landsburg is the master of these kinds of explanations, such as this explanation of the effect of removing trade restrictions; to the extent that I explain these things clearly, I've learned it from Professor Landsburg.[9])

If getting rid of the regulations would be of such unambiguous benefit to Arkansans, why doesn't it happen swiftly? The Arkansas barbering case illustrates the politics of concentrated benefits and dispersed costs. Getting one or two more haircuts per year and saving (say) $10 a year because haircuts are cheaper is nice, but the people who benefit aren't going to take a day off work and drive to Little Rock over $10 a year. For barbers and barbering schools with potentially thousands of dollars per year on the line, the calculation is a bit different—and hence we have stories about barbers descending on the state capitol to rally in favor of regulations on their industry.

Rallies like these are costly examples of why the struggles over licensing and other regulations are negative-sum. Things might not be so bad if the rules only reduced the number of haircuts and transferred wealth from customers to barbers by keeping prices high. It is costly, however, to obtain the regulations and keep them in place. It's socially costly, just like robbing a record store because the people seeking the rules consume valuable resources (like their time) to secure regulatory privileges.

Consider a barber driving from Fort Smith, Arkansas, to Little Rock to join the protest. Google says it's a 158.6-mile drive that takes about two hours and 17 minutes. Round trip, that's about 320 miles of driving taking about four and a half hours. According to the Bureau of Labor Statistics Occupational Outlook Handbook, barbers, hair-stylists, and cosmetologists earn a median wage of $11.97 per hour.[10] Rounding that to $12 an hour and using the IRS mileage rate of 58 cents per mile to account for wear and tear on the car, that comes to about $240 just for a Fort Smith barber to make the trip.[11] That doesn't even count the amount of time spent planning or attending the protest. Society is worse off to the tune of the haircuts not given, the alternative uses of the gas burned getting to Little Rock for the rally, and the other costs incurred protecting barbers from competitors like enforcing the legislation (government officials do not work for free, after all).

Haircuts are a pretty small part of the average consumer's annual spending, and most of us probably won't notice that much if they're *just a bit more expensive*. Trimming regulation is a golden opportunity for the Natural State to improve Arkansans' lives and get the ball rolling toward serious reform.

# 18

# Yes, You Can Be Too Careful: There is Such Thing as Too Much Safety

"You can never be too careful." Actually, yes, you can, and there is such a thing as too much safety regulation.

Consider an example. The local waterpark is trying to decide whether to have three lifeguards on duty at their wave pool during peak hours instead of two. Should it?

In taking the "You can never be too careful" approach, the answer is obvious, and it might even be obscene to suggest otherwise. If we adopt this principle as our standard, everyone in the pool should have a personal lifeguard. Or two. Or three. After all, *you can never be too careful.* That leads us to an absurd conclusion: *any* increase in wave-pool safety justifies an infinite expenditure. Hence, "You can never be too careful" is a non-starter.

To figure out whether the park should hire another lifeguard, we need to know a few things. First, we need to know what hiring another

---

Carden, Art. 2019. "Yes You Can Be Too Careful." American Institute for Economic Research. March 12.

lifeguard would cost. Second, we need to see how the additional lifeguard would affect the park's expected injury-related liability.

Professional lifeguards are substitutes for personal monitoring. If you know there's another lifeguard on duty, your cost and benefit calculations change, too. People are likely to take more risks if they know there are lifeguards there to bail them out. An extra lifeguard makes carelessness less costly. We can expect people to be more careless.

It's grotesque, some might think, that the park would think about the bottom line when *safety* is at stake. But this is where reputation and pricing come in. Places that cut corners on safety will develop a bad reputation. If they're going to stay in business, they'll need to cut prices. Depending on people's preferences, a market might emerge with an array of different price-and-safety combinations, just like there are many different price-and-quality combinations for basically any good or service.

Think about parental incentives, too. If you take your kids to a pool and there are *no* lifeguards—like at most hotel pools—you have strong incentives to keep a watchful eye on your kids because *you* are the only one there to save them. Add a lifeguard and things change: you can spend a little more time scrolling Facebook and a little less time watching vigilantly to make sure your kids are safe.

Should we require extensive training for people who want to be lifeguards? Maybe, but it makes lifeguards more expensive.

So how should the water park decide? They compare costs and benefits, perhaps not this explicitly but at least implicitly. Suppose adding another hour of lifeguarding will increase safety enough to cut expected injury-related liability by $5 and increase pool revenues by $6 because more people will want to swim at a safer pool. Suppose a firm can hire another hour of lifeguarding for $10. In this case, the additional hour of lifeguarding is a wise buy. The park spends $10 and gets $11 worth of new revenue and lower costs. It's a good deal.

Meanwhile, the park could eliminate all its liability and injury-related risk by simply closing up shop altogether. We don't know whether this will increase public safety on net, of course, because it might direct people toward *even more dangerous* kinds of recreation.

Some readers will recoil in horror at the very idea of comparing costs to benefits before choosing a course of action. "You can't put a price on *safety*," they might say—or you might have heard them say it before.

We do put a price on safety, though: *every action* involves comparing costs and benefits. When you go to the pool or go to the beach, you compare the benefits (exercise and fun in the sun) to the costs (the sadness and costs you would incur from different injuries adjusted for their likelihood).

We go to the beach and swim in the Gulf of Mexico even though we may get eaten by sharks. Just because something is possible doesn't mean it's likely—or worth more than cursory attention.

## 19

# Strangers Help You Avoid Getting Ripped Off

Out of the corner of my eye, I saw my phone flash with a notification from the social media app Nextdoor. I cursed myself for failing to turn off the auto-notification, but I saw the post's title and decided to investigate since I was between tasks. It was a post from a neighbor about an experience with a local company and suggesting that we look elsewhere should we need air conditioning repair.

It was an example of how people in a free society provide quality assurance. Brand names matter, and in this case, the AC company's shoddy service and shady dealing sullied their name in the eyes of everyone who read the post and who will now go to a competitor as a result. Free minds and free speech on free social media platforms mean rapid and sometimes ruthless dissemination of information.

Reputation solves some of the problems transaction costs create. Transaction costs include the costs of establishing *trust*. It's hard to

---

Carden, Art. 2019. "How Do You Know You're Not Getting Ripped Off?" American Institute for Economic Research. August 5.

know that you will *actually* get what is promised when it is promised. Platform services, banks, and retailers are ultimately in the business of reducing transaction costs, including the cost of establishing trust. When you see some brand names, you know you're getting high-quality products (and probably paying premium prices). When you see other brand names, you know you're probably not paying more because what you're getting isn't quite as good as the leading brand.

For many firms, their reputation is their most valuable asset. They will go to great lengths to protect it. In my freshman year of college, several of my friends got shigella. The restaurant that gave it to them didn't last much longer. Even when the offenders don't go bankrupt, the damage to their reputation and their bottom line can be long-lasting and substantial. When I was in sixth grade or so, I remember reading about an e. coli outbreak at a fast-food restaurant in another state. It made quite an impression, I think about that every time I see one of them, and I've still never eaten there.

When I mentioned this to an audience of high schoolers, they all mentioned another restaurant that was ground zero for an e. coli outbreak a few years ago. The hit to their reputation also means a likely blow to their ability to charge higher prices and a definite hit to their ability to sell more meals. All else equal, I will make fewer visits to this place over my lifetime than I would have without the e. coli outbreak and vote with my dollars for businesses that haven't been the source of e. coli outbreaks.

Does it work in *every* instance? It doesn't, but it works pretty well. Adam Smith said there is "a great deal of ruin in a nation" and was under no illusion about flawed and fallen people creating a utopia as a consequence of what he called "the obvious and simple system of natural liberty." As social media shows us all too regularly, the line separating a community from a mob can be thin indeed. Services like Yelp, TripAdvisor, Nextdoor, and others help keep businesses on their best behavior—and they work tolerably, even surprisingly well. Even an episode of *South Park* lampooned the power Yelp reviewers wielded—or tried to wield.

That might damn the market process with faint praise. We all have stories about bad customer service or some way we were wronged by a restaurant, an employer, or a retailer. Isn't it naive to say, "Just leave it to the market?"

I don't think so. When we compare ours to the very best world populated by the very best people, actually-existing markets look pretty bad. They cater to our least beautiful instincts of *self*-love, *self*-preservation, and *self*-advancement, and when Yelp hosts reviews, they aren't doing so because they want to help me like a child trying to tie her shoes. They're helping me because I help them—in this case, by providing content and data.

We get strangers to help us by helping them because we can't be friends and family with *everyone*.[12] Maybe it would be nice if the people at Yelp, Waffle House, and Amazon loved me and thought about me how I love and think about my children and friends, but they have their children and friends. Markets ease cooperation, and cooperating with strangers makes it easier for me to love my friends and family well.

When we say, "Leave it to the market," we're engaging in an explicitly comparative exercise. There are many relevant and possible alternatives, each with its own costs and benefits. As Don Boudreaux reminds us, "The State Is Not a Transcendental Being"—nor is it likely to know what Friedrich Hayek called "the particular circumstances of time and place" that would make it a wise steward of the fruits of our labor.[13]

Unlike licensing boards and elected officials, firms like Yelp get indispensable profit-and-loss signals that tell them whether people think they are doing a good job relative to the alternatives. Network effects and switching costs matter, but competition constrains a platform's ability to abuse its users.

There are all sorts of potential problems in markets where people don't share the same information. At first glance, it looks like someone following his most narrowly conceived self-interest has an almost-overwhelming incentive to lie, cheat, steal, and break promises. The problem with this strategy? People talk—and if you don't manage your firm's reputation carefully, it will hurt your bottom line in the long run.

## 20

# Planning and the Pokemon Problem

Fundamentally, there are two different ways to solve what Tyler Cowen and Alex Tabarrok call "the great economic problem" of getting the most out of our resources. Central planning is one way to do it, where a duly constituted authority decides what gets produced and how. Without private ownership of the means of production and, therefore, free markets for the means of production, the central authority cannot engage in genuinely *economic* calculation.

Markets solve the knowledge problem, and in that way, they are a marvel. In markets, people who don't know and may not necessarily care about one another can cooperate to mutual advantage. If Kaz has a stick and wants a rock and Neeku has a rock and wants a stick, they can swap. Both will be better off, even if Kaz does not care about Neeku's well-being and even if Neeku does not care about Kaz's well-being.

---

Carden, Art. 2020. "Planning and the Pokémon Problem." American Institute for Economic Research. January 16.

As we teach in introductory economics classes, free markets create what the economist Tim Harford calls a "world of truth": We produce the right things. We build them the right way. We make them in the proper proportions. They go to the right people. In experimental settings, people armed with nothing more than their own interests and knowledge about what they are willing to pay (or willing to accept) will bargain their way to an outcome that maximizes gains from trade. The economist Vernon Smith explored and explained this experimentally.

There's a potentially huge problem, though, with the equilibrium model. Not everyone has the same information, and self-interested people can use this to take advantage of the poorly informed.

In a recent discussion with students at my kids' school, we called this the "Pokemon Problem" because of the problems that emerge when older card collectors take advantage of the inexperience and naivete (and poor math skills) of younger collectors.

I remember a short cartoon I saw when I was little in which one kid offered to pay his naive "friend" either a dime or a nickel, and the friend picked the nickel because it was bigger. Fortunately, someone with a better-developed ethical compass stepped in and explained the situation. We can probably all tell stories like that.

We read stories like that pretty regularly. You can probably think of a time when you got sick at a restaurant or heard of a product recall. It's a mistake to conclude from this, however, that markets *per se* are the problem. As Tyler Cowen points out, a lot of the failings people attribute to executives don't happen because they are executives per se but because they are people.

The Bible is pretty clear that all have sinned and fall short of the glory of God; the institutional question, then, concerns finding the arrangements of institutions that do the most to mitigate these problems. It's a common mistake to think that asymmetric information in markets is a bulletproof case for government regulation. After all, governments have lousy incentives and asymmetric information. Moreover, entrepreneurs have come up with a lot of pretty ingenious ways to show that they aren't going to take advantage of short-term asymmetric information.

I told the students that their integrity and their reputations are among their most valuable assets. We see this pretty readily in the marketplace, where firms hustle to protect their brand names. People talk a lot—and one way to lose a lot of business is to provide lousy products at high prices. Markets help you know you're not getting ripped off by embedding a lot of information in brand names and reputations. The Bible says a good name is better than great riches. In a market economy, a good name can lead to great riches.

In books published in 2011 and 2018, the economist David Rose explains the importance of a society's moral foundation. Societies of short-sighted opportunists will not prosper, while those who have taught truth-telling and honesty norms will tend to do better. One might not only want to do the right thing because it is right. One might also want to do the right thing because it is good business. People solve the Pokemon problem and show that they are potential trading partners who won't take advantage of others by tending to their reputations.

# 21

# Why Can You Trust Strangers With Candy?

Everyone knows the story: *never* take candy from a stranger. Or get in the car with a stranger. Or make eye contact with a stranger. After all, you don't know who they are. They're *strangers*. They are *other*, outside the tribe, not among our regular contacts. Their intentions may not be honorable.

And yet there I was, at my son's birthday party, staring at a table littered with candy we had taken from strangers that we were planning to give to our kids and their friends. Even where we knew who had made the finished good—my wife and kids had baked and decorated the birthday cake—there are strangers at every turn along the path from raw and naked earth to the cake before us. The eggs, milk, flour, and sugar that went into the cake? Strangers bought them from other strangers before selling them to us. My family used spoons and scrapers made by strangers and bought from strangers to mix all the ingredients.

---

Carden, Art. 2020. "It's Not Regulation that Keeps Your Food Safe" American Institute for Economic Research. June 22.

They baked the cake in an oven made by strangers. They colored the icing with an unholy mix of chemicals made by strangers. And those strangers rely for their daily bread on still other armies of strangers.

It's remarkable. If you have a sweet tooth, you take candy from strangers *all the time*. If you've ridden in a cab or with Uber or Lyft, you've gone against the advice of your mother and the other people who love you and have gotten in the car with a *stranger*. You probably didn't bat an eye. Why not?

It's a classic problem: strangers have weak incentives to honor their promises. They may never see you again, after all, so they don't suffer meaningful consequences from deceiving you. In his famous article about the lemons market, the economist and Nobel laureate George Akerlof showed how asymmetric information could cause cooperation to unravel.

And yet it doesn't, at least not entirely—and it's robust enough for us to stagger along getting a little better from day to day and year to year. How?

Entrepreneurs do it. It's not necessarily because they care about you, *per se*. It's because they care about themselves and their loved ones: those around them who are very much *not* strangers in their eyes. When you look at a firm's valuable assets, its most valuable asset is probably its reputation. After all, if they screw you over, you probably won't be back. The more competitive markets are, the more likely it is that you will be able to find a substitute. Strangers with candy earn your repeat business because they *don't* poison you—strangers who do tend to get tarnished reputations and lower profits.

"It's because of regulation." Not mainly. Regulation can solve information problems, but we live in a world of Yelp reviews, social media, and news outlets looking for *any* story, no matter how trivial. Reputation is in the driver's seat. In any case, regulation creates a curiously-messed-up food environment in which it's harder to enter the food service market. Therefore people eat more meals prepared at home than they otherwise would. Pathogens flourish in home kitchens, many of which, I suspect, would not pass health department inspections. If you believe people are wise and responsible enough to clean their kitchens, think it possible they can make decent choices about restaurants and candy.

Should you trust strangers with candy? If the stereotypical mustachioed, windowless-van-driving weirdo approaches you, then it's probably a good idea to say "no thank you"—and maybe call the cops, though whether the cops will do anything about it is an open question (we're still "waiting" for resolution from when our house was broken into in 2008, for example). There are multiple layers of redundancy in the candy market, all driven by reputation, that provide the assurance you might want from the products you buy. When you unwrap a Kit Kat or Snickers bar, the biggest threat to your health comes from the sugar and not from the likelihood that it is tainted.

So enjoy—in moderation. The strangers are looking out for you, and they are all too happy to do so. Why? Because by looking out for *you*, they look out for the non-strangers in their lives.

# PART IV

# How *Not* To Help Strangers

## 22

# Drop Your Phone

I'm something of a klutz. It was evident when I was at the gym and dropped my phone. The phone landed just so, and the edge bent in just such a way as to make it irreparable. If I wanted a phone, I was going to have to buy a new one. I had declined Apple Care coverage when I'd picked up the new phone a couple of weeks before, so this was going to be a pretty substantial hit ($438 after tax, in fact). That I was paying so much to replace a two-week-old phone stung quite a bit.

*But,* you might respond, *it was terrible for you, but it's good for the economy. After all, it created work for the person who checked you in at the Apple store, not to mention the people at the Genius Bar who helped you evaluate your old phone and get a new one. And need we highlight the people involved throughout the process, from mining to manufacturing to distributing to accounting? By breaking your phone, you're creating opportunities for people who analyze supply chains and operations. If no one ever broke their phone, we wouldn't need anyone to explore inventory management practices to ensure that they have the right*

---

Carden, Art. 2019. "My Busted iPhone Did Not Help the Economy." American Institute for Economic Research. October 22.

number of phones on hand at any given moment. 'Twas a curse for you, but a blessing insofar as it encouraged the national labor.

That's a superficially appealing story if you listen to how people report on and discuss natural disasters and wars' economic effects. It's misleading, though, because it doesn't think past Stage One, to use Thomas Sowell's way of putting it in the subtitle to his book *Applied Economics: Thinking Beyond Stage One.* The argument above is a straightforward indulgence of the Broken Window Fallacy, named for the example that started Frederic Bastiat's "That Which is Seen and That Which is Not Seen." It only considers what is immediate and obvious—what is seen—and it ignores what is remote and opaque but no less real—what is not seen.

My broken iPhone was 100% tragedy with no silver lining. Let me count the ways: first, there's the time I spent driving to and from the Apple store. I was taking up valuable road space—during rush hour, no less—as I needed to get my phone fixed or replaced as I had an out-of-town trip the next day. Second, I burned gas that I otherwise could have used for something fun like a family trip to Six Flags or for something boring like getting to and from work. Third, I burned a lot of time I otherwise could have spent doing something else, like exercising (believe me, I need it).

The costs don't stop there. The Apple Store is a busy place with a lot going on. I've taken several of their "Today at Apple" classes, and their associates spend a lot of time helping people figure out how their products work. The time and attention they had to spend helping me was time and attention they could have spent helping people learn how to take better photos, organize their documents, or turn their iProduct on and connect it to a wireless network. All of that goes up in the figurative smoke of my broken iPhone and the time we spent replacing it.

Then there's the $438 I spent on the phone itself. $400 went to Apple, and $38 went to various taxing authorities. My mind boggles when I think of the other things I could have done with that $438. I could have bought a plane ticket and gone to visit my sister in Minneapolis. I could have bought a plane ticket and gone to visit my other sister in Houston. I could have taken my family out for several *very* nice meals. If you've never been, Birmingham, Alabama is a fantastic food city: a couple of years ago, Highlands Bar & Grill *finally* won the James Beard Award, which is kind of like the Oscars for restaurants, and there are a lot of other excellent places to eat. Alas, we had to forego all that because I spent the money replacing my phone. I could have bought a new suit or a new pair of shoes or some books, which would have filled the pockets of the tailor, the cobbler, or the bookseller. I could have just saved the money and not spent it, in which case it would have left resources available for a business that needs to finance an investment—an investment in iPhones for its staff, perhaps.

Had I not broken the phone, then I would have "iPhone + something awesome." Having broken the phone, though, all I have is "iPhone"—or more accurately, "iPhone+regret." The world is worse off to the tune of whatever else I could have done with the money I spent replacing my phone.

*But surely something good came of it. Didn't it inspire you to write this article?* It did, and as luck would have it, I broke my phone shortly before the semester started and therefore had a fresh example I could discuss with my class. As the father of three children, though, if there's *anything* I have in super-abundance, it's real-life examples I can use to draw on the unseen costs of broken windows (three of them are literally about broken windows). As for this article, had I not broken my phone, I probably would have written about something else.

It all seems obvious when you think about it: the world is worse off to the tune of what I *didn't* spend $438 doing. However, the problem is that a lot of people don't think about it and instead indulge popular-but-wrong claims about multiplier effects. This thinking—or more accurately, this unthinking—pervades the popular understanding of natural disasters, wars, taxes, stadium subsidies, arts subsidies, and all sorts of other things that amount at best to a mere redirection of resources.

If the story has a moral, it's this: you should probably just be more careful with scarce resources that have alternative uses. I know I plan to be.

## 23

# Be a Socialist

I share a lot of the concerns and goals of those who describe themselves as "socialists." More health care and housing for poor people? Great. More educational opportunities for the least well-off? Absolutely. A cleaner environment? Sure thing. Gender and racial equality? Immediately, please.

Why, then, am I not a *socialist*? As political and economic ideas go, it's So Hot Right Now. It's also cross-generational as political superstars Bernie Sanders and Alexandria Ocasio-Cortez refer to themselves as "democratic socialists."

I think, though, that they are making serious mistakes. To put it simply, people too often mistake the ends for the means and define economic and political systems in terms of their advocates' stated goals rather than those systems' actual characteristics. There is a lot more standing between the self-described socialists and their visions than a failure of political will. In the early 20th century, we saw that socialism doesn't work in theory. The fall of the Berlin Wall and the collapse

---

Carden, Art. 2019. "Why I am Not a Socialist." American Institute for Economic Research. July 9.

of the Soviet Union provided decisive evidence in the late 20th century that it doesn't work in practice. If questions remain as the USSR fades into the historical distance, resource-rich Venezuela's freefall into chaos, poverty, and repression should answer them.

To borrow from Thomas Sowell, I think we should define economic systems in terms of the social processes they set in motion. It isn't enough to speak and write in terms of intentions. It is especially true when we find ourselves emptily and airily advocating things no decent person would oppose. Robert Heilbroner defines socialism as "a centrally planned economy in which the government controls all means of production." According to Ludwig von Mises (1949), "The essential mark of socialism is that *one will* alone act."

That "one will" might be a dictator or the chair of an elected committee of central planners (for short, let's just call it "the state"). Rather than a multitude of wills enacting disparate plans, socialism features a *single* will enacting a *single*, all-encompassing plan.

At first glance, it seems reasonable. Why not replace the chaos of the unfettered market where people regularly make poor decisions, entrepreneurs often screw up, and more money means more votes with something far more just, orderly, and scientific? Mises answers by asking the fundamental question: "Can a socialist system operate as a system of the division of labor?"

His answer: no, it cannot.

He initially made the argument in 1920 in an article called "Economic Calculation in the Socialist Commonwealth," expanded the discussion into *Socialism: An Economic and Sociological Analysis*, and restated it in a section on non-market cooperation in *Human Action*, his magnum opus. Socialists tried and failed to rescue their system from his critique, and, for a long time, people (many economists included) mistakenly believed that Mises and Friedrich Hayek, who had discarded his youthful socialism on encountering Mises's arguments, had lost the debate. Ultimately, however, theory and practice vindicated them.

What, exactly, was their argument? Here's how I read it.

Mises stacked the deck against himself by assuming away all the easy objections to socialism. He assumed that the central planner was utterly uncorrupted by any consideration other than the well-being of society. He assumed further that the central planner had a menu of technological possibilities, available resources, and the people's preferences. The central planner knew precisely the pattern of consumers' goods that would maximize welfare. Arranging society's factors of production to produce everything with maximal efficiency was his only job. He only has to do so without using market prices determined by the voluntary exchange of privately owned means of production.

It is impossible. Note that Mises (and Hayek after him) doesn't say, "It's difficult." He claims that the central planner can't compare the costs and benefits of different ways of producing society's array of consumers' goods without private ownership and prices generated by market exchange. There are a few steps from private ownership to rational economic calculation:

**1. Private ownership**. Individual owners have the right to use, alienate, or derive income from the means of production like land and capital. As residual claimants to the income the means of production generates, they have stronger incentives to use them wisely than does a member of a central-planning board or larger polity who bears no personal cost from choosing poorly.

**2. Exchange**. People can exchange privately owned means of production. Exchange gives a practical outlet to disagreement, which is an unavoidable fact of the human condition. Imagine your neighbor owns a farm on the outskirts of town. You disagree with her and think the land should become a shopping center. When the means of production are privately owned, you can act on your conviction by finding someone willing to finance your venture, buying the farm, and converting it into a shopping center.

**3. Prices**. Prices emerge from market exchange and provide, at any point in time, people's best estimate of the value of a tool, tractor, ounce of copper, or plot of land in its best available use. The information is crucial, and once again, if you think the pattern of prices is wrong, you can go into the market and buy what you think is undervalued or sell short what you think is overvalued. Your action contributes valuable knowledge that helps future buyers and sellers compare their estimates of the value of the means of production to everyone else's.

**4. Profits and Losses**. The proof of the pudding is in the eating. The proof of the plan is in the profits and losses. If you have chosen wisely, the market rewards you with a profit, which is an increment above everyone else's assessment of the best possible uses of the means of production. It's a pat on the back from the invisible hand, and it's the market's way of rewarding your judgment by increasing the means at your disposal. If you have chosen poorly, the market punishes you with a loss. It's a slap in the face from the invisible hand, and it's the market's way of punishing you for wasting resources by decreasing the means at your disposal.

As Mises argues, prices, profits, and losses are crucial. So is the market's institutional structure. The planning board's instruction to mimic what the market does but do it more efficiently is curious. As Mises puts it, "They want people to play market as children play war, railroad, or school. They do not comprehend how such childish play differs from the real thing it tries to imitate." Later, he describes how the market process revolutionizes production means and methods: "The capitalist system is not a managerial system; it is an entrepreneurial system."

Mises's critics responded that they owed him a debt of gratitude for showing that prices are essential to economic calculation. Still, they argued that market exchange of private property was not necessary because they could derive prices for the means of production from a mathematical model. In 1945, however, Friedrich Hayek argued in his classic essay "The Use of Knowledge in Society" that this is true *if* we define the economic problem as one of solving *known* equations subject to *known* inventories of inputs and *known* constraints. Unfortunately, some interpreted this as a concession on Hayek's part: central planning *could* calculate, after all—it was just inefficient relative to the price mechanism.

Hayek made a different argument, though. He argued that the economic problem is of a very different kind that a planner cannot solve with a big-enough computer. He argues that it is a problem of assembling, combining, and deploying knowledge distributed across many people and available to no single mind. As Mises argued earlier, it is a problem that cannot be solved by a central planner, no matter what the computational resources at his disposal. The information needed to solve it (prices, profits, and losses) emerges from individual, purposive action—in this case, buying and selling ownership of the means of production in markets. The knowledge that emerges is unavailable to any planner or anyone else through any other mechanism (and indeed, as he and others pointed out, to the extent that the Soviet Union was able to "calculate" it was able to do so by observing prices in places with markets for the means of production).

Empirically, the socialist record is one of dismal and at times murderous failure. Why, then, do intellectuals, scholars, and commentators continue in their romantic attachment to it? In a summary of Hayek's contributions, Peter Saunders (2007) puts it this way: "Hayek understood that capitalism offends intellectual pride, while socialism flatters it." Mises understood this, too, and he worked tirelessly to answer those who thought themselves fit to plan for others, or at least to select those who would plan for others. Even though I agree with socialists on many social goals, I think the record of theory and history shows that socialist planning is an impossible task.

## 24
## Be a Communist

On May 1, 1886, some 300,000 workers around the United States took direct action and went on strike, demanding an "Eight-hour day with no cut in pay." The date had initially been proposed in 1884 by the Federation of Organized Trades and Labor Unions.

Two days later, violence between workers and police at McCormick Reaper Works in Chicago led to a rally at Haymarket Square on May 4.[14] The Americans' eight-hour workday movement launched a global campaign to celebrate May 1 of every year as International Workers' Day. In the United States, "Labor Day" is celebrated in September to separate it from the socialist and communist origins of May 1 as the date for International Workers' Day.

It seems like support for socialism should have crumbled like the Berlin Wall in 1989 or shredded like the Iron Curtain in 1991, yet here we are a mere three decades later, roughly, with renewed and rising

---

Carden, Art. 2020. "A May Day Remembrance." American Institute for Economic Research. May 1.

interest in socialism around the world. Henry Hazlitt was right: people need to relearn the good ideas every generation.

Socialism is both: it is a bad idea, and it is intuitive. It is intuitive because it evokes what seems like noble aspirations. Who *doesn't* want to see the hungry fed and the naked clothed? Families socialize people, and they are small socialist enterprises governed by the principle of "from each according to his ability, to each according to his needs." Central authorities (the parents) make production and allocation decisions, and the strong provide for the weak. Socialism appeals to our innate sense of fairness. It also appeals to our desires for comfort, safety, and protection. Very importantly, it also appeals to our desire to protect others from want and oppression. Socialism appeals to the familial instincts that make us leap to the defense of our children and siblings.

It tugs at our heartstrings, but socialism fails every time societies try it. It doesn't fail because the people aren't worthy of the system. It fails because it is fundamentally, cripplingly, and irredeemably broken at its most basic conceptual level.

To be sure, a great many communists have been butchers. In his foreword to a reissue of Eugen Richter's *Pictures of the Socialistic Future*, Bryan Caplan (2010) argues, following Richter, that "the (socialist) movement was born bad. While the early socialists were in fact 'idealists,' their ideal was totalitarianism." in a 2019 EconLog post, he quotes one Cuban revolutionary's "one-page hop from bleeding heart to mailed fist," first explaining how his heart bleeds for the illiterate and then a few sentences later suggesting that Fidel "have an incinerator dug about 40 or 50 meters deep, and every time one of those obstinate cases [of delinquency] came up, to drop the culprit in the incinerator, douse him with gasoline, and set him on fire" to "make an example of him for future generations."

However, socialism cannot be fixed or solved or implemented smoothly merely by putting the right people—the right kind of idealists, presumably the non-totalitarian kind—in charge. Ludwig von Mises's "Economic Calculation in the Socialist Commonwealth" was first published 100 years ago, in 1920. Mises argued that even if we peopled the socialist commonwealth with omnipotent, entirely benevolent angels, it would still "fail" in that there would be no way to evaluate alternative production methods in the absence of the prices necessary for monetary calculation. Meaningful prices, in turn, could only emerge in a setting where people are voluntarily trading private ownership of the means of production. Economic "calculation" in the absence of prices, profits, and losses becomes, as Mises argues, a fundamentally arbitrary groping-about-in-the-dark that tends not toward order and prosperity but disorder and poverty.

In his article "The Use of Knowledge on Society," Friedrich Hayek emphasized how and why socialism would not work. He pointed out that the economic problem—what "we wish to solve when we try to construct a rational economic order"—is not that posited by the defenders of socialism. Their solution follows readily from their assumptions: with perfect information about the stocks of productive factors, consumers' preferences, and the menu of possible technologies, "the problem which remains is purely one of logic." However, he points out, "(t)his, however, is emphatically *not* the economic problem which society faces." As he continues,

> "The peculiar character of the problem of a rational economic order is determined precisely by the fact that the knowledge of the circumstances of which we must make use never exists in concentrated or integrated form but solely as the dispersed bits of incomplete and frequently contradictory knowledge which all the separate individuals possess. The economic problem of society is thus not merely a problem of how to allocate 'given' resources—if 'given' is taken to mean given to a single mind

which deliberately solves the problem set by these 'data.' It is rather a problem of how to secure the best use of resources known to any of the members of society, for ends whose relative importance only these individuals know. Or, to put it briefly, it is a problem of the utilization of knowledge which is not given to anyone in its totality."

This passage reminds me of something John Maynard Keynes wrote about the wholly private economy: it is only by "accident or design" that it would wind up at full employment. One of the problems with socialism is that if it were, by some miracle, to settle upon the most efficient specialization and production patterns, it would have to be by accident.

The inescapable conclusion of the Mises-Hayek argument about socialist calculation is that people cannot design an efficient socialist society. The "dispersed bits of incomplete and frequently contradictory knowledge" are rendered legible by voluntary market exchange. As Kristian Niemietz documents in his 2019 book *Socialism: The Failed Idea that Never Dies*, central planners cannot solve the problem whether they are wearing velvet gloves or mailed gauntlets.[15]

The specter of communism haunted Europe when Marx and Engels published *The Manifesto of the Communist Party* in 1848. A related specter haunts Europe and the rest of the West today, only it is a milder specter that we call "democratic socialism." Better than totalitarian communism of the Stalinist or Maoist variety? Definitely, but this is to damn it with faint praise. Socialism of any kind, no matter how implemented and how noble its advocates, is destined to fail.

## 25

# Spend a Ton of Money on "Black Friday"

With Black Friday upon us, here's something important to remember: you're not "helping the economy" by spending intemperately and making imprudent impulse purchases. You're just spending intemperately and being imprudent. There's nothing *inherently* wrong with that. Maybe you have a very high time preference such that you want stuff now now *now* and are willing to sacrifice future consumption for it, or perhaps it's part of an occasional and considered splurge a few times a year.

You shouldn't excuse yourself or think there's a silver lining in extra consumption because you're not "helping" the economy more than if you simply saved the money (where people could lend it to people who are expanding our productive capacity) or stuffed it in a mattress (where its removal from circulation would reduce prices).

---

Carden, Art. 2019. "You Are Harming No One or Anything by Not Spending on Black Friday." American Institute for Economic Research. November 28.

It's hard to appreciate if you only account for what you see during the holiday season. I took my oldest child to Walmart near the end of the day on Thanksgiving once. I don't think I had been Black Friday shopping since working at a music store in high school, but this was a lot of fun. We weren't there for anything (we bought oranges if I remember correctly). We were just there to observe. And observe we did, joyfully and peacefully (and pleasantly surprised by gratis cookies and coffee). There weren't any brawls that would end up on YouTube. For the most part, things were orderly. The salespeople were in good spirits, and they had roped off a path through the store with a map to where all the hottest items were. Everyone seemed happy.

In this light, it seems hard to believe that indulgent spending doesn't stimulate the economy. What about the paradox of thrift, which says that if we all save more (individually rational), reducing spending will lead to lower overall output and employment (socially irrational)? A sudden increase in saving will cause a reorganization of the economy, but as Friedrich Hayek argued in his criticism of the Keynesian framework in which the paradox of thrift plays a central role, "Mr. Keynes's aggregates conceal the most fundamental mechanisms of change."[16]

Or, as I've heard Peter J. Boettke put it, most (highly aggregated) macroeconomics is an effort to do economics without prices. Prices change, though. While a derived-demand effect dominates for the Walmarts and Targets of the world, an interest rate effect dominates for firms (like mining concerns) with operations far from final consumption.

In his 1994 book *Ethics and Economic Progress,* James M. Buchanan explores the "ethical content" of "puritan virtues" like the work ethic and the saving ethic. Buchanan argues that, in a world where an ever-finer division of labor determines productivity, we are *all* better off by our standards when we work more and save more. Hence, he argues, we developed (albeit unintentionally) ethics of hard work and saving that have helped us capture at least some of these gains.

By Buchanan's logic, refraining from impulsive consumption is prudent not because material riches are not the same as moral riches (while this is true, Buchanan's focus is more narrow) but because by our standards for private consumption, we get higher standards of living if we all save more. The collective action problem is, of course, enormous. However, strong work and saving ethics help us capture at least some of the gains.

Here, then, is what you should think about as you celebrate Thanksgiving and get ready to go Black Friday shopping: you aren't necessarily stimulating the economy or making anyone better off with that impulse purchase. Don't feel bad for refraining from that purchase, and, importantly, don't try to justify your impulse purchase with a story about how you're taking one for the team and stimulating the economy.

Of course, if you *want* that bauble, buy it. Do so boldly and unapologetically because you and your preferences matter, too. Know this, though: if you decide to refrain and save the money, your newfound puritan prudence will, in the long run, benefit everyone else through higher economic growth.

## 26

# Refuse to Use Self-Checkout To Save Jobs

Have you seen a meme exhorting you not to use self-checkout because it impoverishes workers who are replaced by unfeeling scanners? There is no harm in making that choice. But if we remember our lessons from Frederic Bastiat, we can see why the rationale behind the campaign is absurd.

After all, why should we stop with the self-checkout? We would create more jobs if we didn't even select our groceries but instead hired personal shoppers to do it for us. To some extent, this is what companies like Instacart and Shipt do already, but the shoppers aren't charged with making all your decisions. They just pick up the groceries and drive them to your house—and maybe they even use the self-checkout.

We could go one better. Instead of driving yourself to the grocery store, you should take a chauffeured car. Or, if you care about creating jobs, you should hire a team of people to carry you in a sedan chair

---

Carden, Art. 2019. "Don't Feel Bad About Using the Self Checkout." American Institute for Economic Research. July 19.

and then a small army of assistants to move your items one by one once you've shopped.

Of course not. Carrying a person several miles undoubtedly burns a lot of calories, which means you'll have to spend a lot to maintain your entourage of assistants. This, in turn, will encourage the national labor as more farmers and retailers are required to produce the sustenance your assistants require. It creates loads of white-collar jobs, too, as you would no doubt need to provide health benefits for your assistants, have your sedan chair insured, and so on.

And then again, if you cared about creating jobs, you would hire a mastication service to send someone to your house, chew your food for you, and then spit it into your mouth like a mother bird feeding its babies. You're already willing to sacrifice convenience in the name of creating jobs. Is it too much to ask that you forsake hygiene and dignity?

Of course, this is absurd. You're not spreading prosperity when you choose the labor-intensive option just because it's labor-intensive. You're wasting resources.

If we cared about jobs for cashiers and baggers, we'd do away with rules that make labor more expensive. A lot of the benefit of a bad job at a low wage is that it provides invaluable labor market experience and, perhaps, connections that might help you succeed later. The rich and the middle class don't need low-wage jobs because they are likely embedded in denser networks that can provide them with connections and opportunities to shake hands with influential people. The poor aren't so lucky.

You should save time and money by using the self-service checkout kiosk if that's what works for you, and do so guilt-free. If you're worried about people losing jobs, don't.

A quick search turned up this 2017 claim that millennials spent $237 per month on groceries.[17] Go ahead and assume that's accurate, and assume that these millennials save 1% on their grocery bill every month thanks to the self-checkout. That comes to just about $25 a year. It doesn't sound like much, but what would you do with an extra $25? Here are a few options that will help you see how you're not "destroying jobs" by using the self-checkout—and conversely, how you're not "creating jobs" by conspicuously wasting money and other valuable resources:

First, you could take that $25 and you could spend it. This much is obvious. Maybe you get another haircut and create an opportunity for a cosmetologist to pick up a few extra dollars.

Second, you could save it. By leaving the $25 unconsumed, you leave it for someone else to borrow and put to productive use. *Your individual $25 might not be that important, but when a banker pools it with a bunch of other people's $25 in additional savings, it might be enough to finance a productive venture like a sports bar or a lawn service or new hotel construction.*

Third, you could light it on fire. Actually, destroying US currency might bring criminal penalties, so perhaps you could do something less severe, like sticking it in a mattress or burying it in the yard. Congratulations: you've just made prices lower for everyone else and redistributed your wealth equally by making everyone else's dollars just a bit more valuable.

As an economist, I can't tell you exactly what to do. I don't know your values, preferences, and so on. I *can*, however, tell you that if you're conspicuously wasting resources, then you're doing just that: wasting resources. Don't give in to social pressure, use the self-checkout if you wish, and don't lose any sleep over what your friends share in their social media feeds.

*Speaking of Social Media, I was inspired here by something Steve Horwitz shared. If you want to learn economics from memes, I humbly suggest my page* Economics in One Meme.

## 27

# Advocate Higher Taxes

A group of billionaires—16 who have identified themselves, and one who has chosen to remain anonymous—got some attention in 2019 for their open letter calling for higher taxes on high incomes and huge fortunes like theirs. Maybe it's a noble sentiment, but what makes us think paying higher taxes is especially virtuous in a world with so many alternatives?

Given its track record, it's not at all clear to me that the U.S. government—or my state, county, or local government—would be a wise steward of any money I feel like I don't need. You know those bumper stickers that say something like "It will be a great day when schools have all the money they need and the army has to hold a bake sale to buy a tank," or something like that? I'm not sure I want more of my money going to an entity that spends so much on tanks and bombs.

You can probably see the dilemma. Governments at all levels take our money and do some good things (roads, basic science) and some

---

Carden, Art. 2019. "Government Is Not a Wise Steward." American Institute for Economic Research. July 3.

bad things (wars, ethanol subsidies). I'm not sure they're going to be good stewards of the money they might take from others—and perhaps eventually from us if the history of the income tax and its downward drift is instructive.

Should they give it to charity? Maybe. Even then, the decision isn't quite as clear-cut. There are nonprofits that seem to exist strictly to raise funds, not to solve any problems, as Tyler Cowen points out in his book *Big Business: A Love Letter to an American Anti-Hero*. Even if we address the possibility that we end up joining a scam like the Bluth Foundation's battle against TBA in the series *Arrested Development*, Yoram Barzel (1974) famously argued that it is very difficult to give away money in a way that benefits the people we are trying to help. Even for the devoted humanitarian with resources like GiveWell at her disposal, "Give your money to charity" wouldn't obviously deliver maximal bang for one's benevolent buck.

This raises yet another option, which would be some variation on "Just leave it in the bank." Park it in the stock market where it will earn returns, and reinvest the earnings in ever-more-productive assets with which we can raise our standards of living.

So what should people do? It's a terribly hard problem without an easy solution. Indeed, I would suggest it's a problem that doesn't have a "solution" at all. For just about any proposition, there's a passage in Adam Smith that's insightful and illuminating, and this case is no different. Here's Smith in a famous passage from *The Wealth of Nations*:

> What is the species of domestic industry which his capital can employ, and of which the produce is likely to be of the greatest value, every individual, it is evident, can, in his local situation, judge much better than any statesman or lawgiver can do for him. The statesman who should attempt to direct private people in what manner they ought to employ their capitals would

not only load himself with a most unnecessary attention, but assume an authority which could safely be trusted, not only to no single person, but to no council or senate whatever, and which would nowhere be so dangerous as in the hands of a man who had folly and presumption enough to fancy himself fit to exercise it.

Part of being human is having a nearly endless number of ways we can think of for others to spend their time, their talent, and their treasure. However, we don't have knowledge of another's "local situation" sufficient to do much more than offer advice. If some of the super-duper-rich think the very best use of their money is to give it to the government, that's their prerogative. They owe it to others, however, to respect their liberty to choose otherwise

## 28

# Boycott Things Made By Strangers You Want to Help

The U.S. women's national team brought home their second consecutive World Cup on the same day that the U.S. men's national team lost in the CONCACAF Gold Cup final to Mexico.

The U.S. women's team, which began the 2019 World Cup with a 13-0 bludgeoning of an overmatched Thailand team (and endured a bit of criticism for so joyfully celebrating late goals in a game they had clearly already won), had a brilliant run through the World Cup tournament and made it look too easy at times.

I watched or at least followed most of the games and got to see a couple of minutes of the final on a big TV near One World Trade Center. The U.S. women's team is clearly the best the world has to offer.

The U.S. men's team is ... not. And yet the men make more money, which a lot of people think is a serious injustice. What if we reacted the

---

Carden, Art. 2019. "To Help Women, Should We Boycott Women's Soccer?" American Institute for Economic Research. July 14.

way a lot of activists want us to react when they see workers they think are being unjustly exploited and boycotted the product?

Let's just try a mental experiment. Let's regard the players on the team as some seem to regard themselves, exploited and underpaid. The same claims are made for many people around the world. The commonly proposed solution is the boycott.

Think about this. Would we help the members of the U.S. women's national team (and female athletes more generally) by *refusing* to go to games, *refusing* to buy their merch, *refusing* to watch them on TV, and so on on the grounds that we will only buy a scarf and change the channel back to the USWNT when we see that they're being paid better?

No—not if you understand why boycotting clothing companies that employ "sweatshop" labor and food companies that employ low-wage migrant fruit pickers would be counterproductive.

A lot of the commentary has focused on the fact that the women's national team works just as hard as the men (if not harder) and wins championships while the men struggle and fail to qualify for the 2018 World Cup. They're the best in the world, I enjoy watching them, and I'm proud of their achievement. However, merely working hard and being very good at something is insufficient. You have to work hard and be very good at something people are willing to pay you to do.

Suppose you're one of the best kazoo players in the world. You might not earn as much as a mediocre accountant because, for whatever reason, there's a much larger market for accountants—even mediocre ones—than there is for professional kazoo virtuosos. To use another example, male models probably work as hard as female models, but they're paid much less.[18]

In this light, U.S women's national team (USWNT) superstar Megan Rapinoe hit the nail on the head when Rachel Maddow asked her what fans can do to increase players' incomes: go to the games, buy the gear, and watch them on TV.

In other words, increase demand for their services. Raise the value of their marginal products. The National Women's Soccer League (NWSL) apparently streams its games on Yahoo Sports, if you're looking for a way to contribute to higher demand for women's sports. Tune in, and encourage your friends to do the same. Higher salaries will follow.

By contrast, boycotting and refusing to watch the USWNT and the NWSL would almost certainly hurt the players. They compete in an insanely competitive market for entertainment, not just on the soccer field. If people were to stop watching, how long would they last? Similarly, what do you think happens to low-wage workers in sweatshops when there's suddenly no longer any demand for their product? They don't earn higher incomes, if that's what you're wondering.

In competitive markets, the intersection of workers' productivity and their best available alternatives determine their incomes. Hence, the way to increase their incomes is to make them more productive, give them better options, or both.

Think about the demand side. Revenue from the last cycle for the men's World Cup was over $6 billion, which is almost *46 times* as much as the $131 million anticipated for the women's World Cup cycle, 2019–22. Much has been made of the fact that *game* revenue from ticket sales and such for USWNT games was higher than game revenue for USMNT games.[19]

This hasn't been true from year to year, though, and gate revenue is only part of the story. Given that sponsorships and payments for TV rights for U.S. Soccer aren't earmarked "for the men's team" or "for the women's team," it's difficult to say with any confidence that the value of the marginal product for women's-soccer players is higher than the value of the marginal product for men's-soccer players.

What's more, women's-soccer players got a larger share of the revenue generated by the Women's World Cup than men got from the

Men's World Cup.[20] If there's an injustice here, it's hardly obvious. If you want to close the earnings gap between men and women, you should spend more on women's soccer.

You should also work to improve the players' options off the field. There is a much larger market for male athletes in general than there is for female athletes in general, and those alternatives mean that everything else equal, it's harder to induce men to choose soccer over other sports. A man with the athletic chops to be a world-class soccer player could have likely earned a decent living playing another sport.

Think, for example, about Tim Tebow and Michael Jordan taking up professional baseball—or think about Heisman Trophy winner Kyler Murray, the #1 pick in the 2019 NFL draft and the #9 pick in the 2018 MLB draft. There just aren't as many options out there for women's-soccer players. In order to increase the earnings of women's-soccer players, then, perhaps you should also reallocate some of your entertainment spending toward professional softball.

Who *ultimately* decides how much Megan Rapinoe and company are paid? As Ryan McMaken points out, it's ultimately the consumers, and by and large, consumers have voted overwhelmingly for men's sports.[21] There's a lesson in here, incidentally, about raising the wages of *anyone* we think is underpaid or otherwise ill-used, whether they be sweatshop garment workers, migrant fruit pickers, or the greatest soccer players in the world. If we want them to earn more, we need to vote for them with our dollars.

## 29

# Stop Strangers From Crossing Borders

I've long said that I've never regretted reading anything by Thomas Sowell. It has always, in my estimation, been time well spent. I would say the same thing about Bryan Caplan: his books—*The Myth of the Rational Voter*, *Selfish Reasons to Have More Kids*, and *The Case Against Education*—synthesize piles and piles of important social science and develop novel insights. His blog posts at *EconLog* are always insightful. I'm a proud Caplan fanboy: he is the kind of scholar and the kind of person we should all strive to be.

Caplan is also a world-class nerd who embraces his nerddom and uses it to make the world a better place. He's an aficionado of comic books and graphic novels as well as a passionate and prominent defender of open immigration. In *Open Borders*, which he wrote with cartoonist Zach Weinersmith (of the always-excellent *Saturday Morning Breakfast Cereal*), he offers a (literally and figuratively) colorful defense of the best idea in economic development that no one is really trying. As

---

Carden, Art. 2019. "The Case for Open Borders Is Stronger than You Think." American Institute for Economic Research. November 2.

I've written in several places, the best thing we could do for the poorest people in the world is to make it easy for them to move to where their labor is worth a lot more and where their standards of living would be much higher.

*Open Borders* is an attempt at persuasion. On the surface, the case for open borders is simply overwhelming. As a matter of simple justice, it's not clear why we should prohibit what Robert Nozick called "capitalist acts between consenting adults" just because those consenting adults are on opposite sides of an imaginary line called a border. The economic effects of increased immigration would be simply staggering, as well, with estimates from the economist Michael Clemens suggesting that we can reasonably expect anywhere from a 50 to a 150 percent increase in global output from complete labor market integration. Even if Clemens's estimates are way off, the worst case of plausible scenarios would still shower us with new riches, which Caplan calls "Niagara Falls economics" as opposed to a mere "trickle-down" (p. 37).

After laying out some basic arguments for open borders, Caplan bends over backwards to address the most plausible objections to his argument. He finds them all wanting. Immigrants aren't terribly likely to move the political needle, contrary to the fears of those who think immigrants from poor countries will import the institutions that keep those countries poor. They aren't going to take our jobs or lower our wages. In fact, they will enrich us. They aren't going to destroy our culture. If anything, they will enrich it (sushi burrito, anyone?). Financially, immigrants are a great deal: even for immigrants who might be net fiscal drains, the productivity effect is far larger than the fiscal effect (p. 77). As Caplan and Weinersmith note, people rejoiced when the Berlin Wall came down because it meant so many people could enjoy freedom and prosperity that had been sorely lacking under communism. They didn't say, "The Wall needs to stay up lest our precious liberties die at the hands of a communist horde."

They devote a lot of space to "keyhole solutions" that address people's fears about immigration. Blanket restrictions on immigration are a draconian solution to small problems that can be addressed with well-targeted interventions. If we are worried about immigrants making bad political choices or bleeding the welfare state dry, we could fix this through the tax code. Perhaps immigrants could have to go through a long probationary period before being allowed to vote or before qualifying for government benefits. Perhaps they could be required to pay an "entry fee" of sorts that could then be redistributed to the people who are inevitably made worse off because of immigration. They hasten to add that none of these keyhole solutions are *just* or *fair*, but they are definitely better than the status quo.

Speaking of justice, they argue that immigration restrictions are moral crimes against the least well-off. They invoke a thought experiment by the philosopher Michael Huemer, author of *The Problem of Political Authority*. Huemer asks us to consider Starving Marvin, who is on his way to buy bread when someone intercepts him and turns him away. This isn't the store refusing to sell to him. They want to, but someone comes along and puts himself between Starving Marvin and the store. This, according to Huemer (and Caplan), is tantamount to murder.

We should, Caplan thinks, reframe the issue: Immigration is not charity. It is, rather, "*justice* and *abundance*." Given what we know about the economic effects of immigration, they argue, we should dispense with questions like "How many immigrants can we afford to take?" and "Shouldn't we take care of our own citizens first?" Given the productivity-increasing potential of free global labor markets, these questions don't make any sense.

They also assert that all philosophical roads (utilitarianism, libertarianism, egalitarianism, and so on) lead to open borders. Doing the greatest good for the greatest number? Open the borders. Respecting people's rights to do as they wish so long as they harm no one else? Open the borders. Making the least well-off better off? Open the borders. Maximizing aggregate output? Open the borders. Doing unto others as we would have them do unto us? Open the borders. Not discriminating on the basis of arbitrary criteria? Immigration restrictions *require* us to discriminate against people on the basis of arbitrary criteria.

Caplan is honest throughout about the fact that he doesn't see it persuading people to open the borders anytime soon, but he ends on a message of hope: draconian policy under Donald Trump notwithstanding, support for increased immigration has risen over time. One of Caplan's frequent opponents, Mark Krikorian, has suggested that having him as the face of the open-borders movement would be a godsend to the anti-immigration faction because his loony extremism would discredit immigration enthusiasts.

Borrowing from the Indiana University sociologist Fabio Rojas, Caplan notes that taking open-borders arguments seriously shifts the Overton Window—the range of policies that are being discussed and that just might be possible (pp. 207ff). *Open Borders* is one step in a marginal revolution, so to speak.

As Caplan puts it, "If I can convince you borders should be 90% or 95% or 99% open, there's no need to dwell on our lingering disagreements" (p. 143). I couldn't agree more. Maybe you won't come away from *Open Borders* wholly convinced that we should let literally anyone in who wants to move here, but I think you'll be persuaded that the status quo is moral and economic madness: at the very least, immigration restrictions should be dramatically reduced.

# 30

# Tax Goods Made By Foreign Strangers

Via a friend, I learned of tariffs on tart cherries from Turkey just in time for the days we were going to spend talking about the effects of tariffs in principles of macroeconomics.[22] The new tariffs are making Michigan cherry farmers "celebrate" even though they make Americans poorer on net. Meanwhile, probably 99.9% of the people affected by the tariffs don't know about them, don't care about them, or believe mistakenly that the tariffs are actually good for the American economy.

Why? The tariffs are obviously good for Michigan cherry farmers. They can sell more cherries at higher prices since the tariffs are protecting them from lower-cost Turkish competition. More money goes into their pockets—and according to the conventional wisdom, this makes us all richer because fewer dollars leave the US. Michigan cherry farmers supposedly spend their higher incomes on American-produced goods, which creates a prosperity-boosting ripple effect.

---

Carden, Art. 2019. The Wicked Politics of Cherry Tariffs. American Institute for Economic Research, Sept 27.

At least that's the story a lot of people believe. It's true that less money leaves the US, but it's also true that we expend more resources and get fewer cherries in the bargain. Cherry consumers obey the law of demand, so at the higher, tariff-inflated cherry prices they buy fewer cherries. This includes people who buy cherries by the bag at the grocery store, and it also includes people who make and sell cherry pies and other products that use cherries. American cherry farmers produce a larger share of US cherry consumption, but overall cherry consumption is lower—and we're worse off for it.

Cherry tariffs have a second important effect: we waste resources producing cherries in Michigan that would have been cheaper had we bought them from Turkish farmers. This would have freed up the labor, land, tools, and so on that people are currently using to grow cherries in Michigan so it could be redeployed elsewhere.

"Doing *what*, exactly?" I hear you asking. This is where economics can't be very specific. The highest-value uses of the resources currently being used to grow cherries have to be discovered, and this is where markets are crucial. American consumers who save money on cherries would do something with it, and the resulting pattern of bids and asks would transmit the relevant knowledge about *what* is most valuable *where*.

Suppose the new cherry tariffs cost Americans $1 each, on average. That's $1 they aren't spending on other goods and services like apples, iPhones, haircuts, or oil changes. Think it possible that when your local oil change place has to lay someone off that it might have at least something to do with cherry tariffs.

If it's not $1 people aren't spending, it's $1 people aren't saving. $1 may not seem like much, but when you add that up across over three hundred million Americans, you're talking about real money that isn't available for someone who is applying for a business loan, a mortgage, a home equity line of credit, or something else.

"But what if they don't spend it *or* save it and instead just stuff it in a mattress?" At first glance, this seems like a knock-down argument in favor of tariffs (or, for that matter, private profligacy and government spending). As Steven Landsburg argued in his classic defense of Ebenezer Scrooge, however, taking a dollar out of circulation and stuffing it in a mattress (or burning it) reduces the money supply and, therefore, reduces prices ever so slightly. For this reason, I've heard it suggested only semi-seriously that if Bill Gates *really* wanted to redistribute his fortune, he would sell everything, convert it all into hard cash, and then light it on fire. By so doing, he would be renouncing the claims he might have on the fruit of others' labor and making everyone else's dollars go just a little bit further.

If tariffs are such a terrible idea, why are they so popular? It's clear why they're popular among Michigan cherry farmers and people who depend on the Michigan cherry industry. Cherry tariffs funnel money directly into their pockets. This doesn't explain, however, why the average voter isn't *outraged*. After all, the tariffs have transferred wealth out of *our* pockets, wasted resources that would be better used elsewhere, and reduced the number of tart cherries we are able to enjoy. What gives?

There are two explanations, both having to do with voters' incentives. First, there's the problem of concentrated benefits and dispersed costs. I don't know exactly how much the new tariffs will cost me, but it probably isn't much more than a cup of coffee or a meal. I don't have an incentive to go to the legislative barricades over $5 or $10. Cherry farmers with hundreds of thousands if not millions of dollars on the line, however, have a much stronger incentive to lobby their congressional representatives, make friends at the US Department of Agriculture, and so on. Cherries, cherry pies, cherry jam, and other cherry products are delicious, but my family doesn't spend enough on cherries every year to make it worth our while to lobby for lower cherry tariffs or track the legislation very closely.

Consider a May 8 entry in the *Federal Register* that includes a call for comment: "Tart Cherries Grown in the State of Michigan, et al.; Free and Restricted Percentages for the 2018-19 Crop Year and Revision of Grower Diversion Requirements for Tart Cherries." Curious, I copied and pasted it into Google Docs and discovered that it's almost 6,000 words long. I got down to "it does not trigger the requirements contained in Executive Order 13771," before I decided to do something else. And Executive Order 13771, "Reducing Regulation and Controlling Regulatory Costs," is over 900 words long.

Maybe I'm failing in my civic duty. A better explanation, however, would be that even if I were motivated solely by the purest altruism, there are probably more effective things I could be doing than reading page after page after page of cherry marketing regulations. In the words of economists and political scientists, I'm *rationally ignorant*. In my individual capacity as a citizen, learning a lot about cherry marketing regulation isn't going to do a whole lot to change things—and so I choose to remain largely ignorant of the subtleties and nuances of cherry marketing regulations and do something else with my time.

"Rational ignorance" helps us understand why cherry growers rather than cherry consumers control the flow of legislation and regulation, but it only goes partway. In his 2007 book *The Myth of the Rational Voter: Why Democracies Choose Bad Policies*, Bryan Caplan develops an idea he calls "rational irrationality." Rational irrationality is a kind of rational ignorance carried a step further. As Caplan points out, the usual stories about rational ignorance and the like don't tell us why agricultural subsidies, tariffs, and so on are hugely popular even among the people who are hurt by them. International trade is a perfect example: the average voter likely thinks that the new cherry tariffs will make Americans richer, on net, even though economists have been banging the free-trade drum for about two and a half centuries and even though there is an overwhelming consensus among professional economists that free trade is better for a country than protectionism. In short, most voters hold *irrational* beliefs about international trade: they claim to want prosperity, but they vote enthusiastically for policies like cherry tariffs that make us poorer.

In a twist on the "rational ignorance" explanation, Caplan points out that it's simply expensive to change one's economically irrational beliefs. First, there is a social cost: if all your friends think cherry tariffs will Make America Great Again, then it could be socially awkward to be the person who is jumping into the conversation with "*actually...*" followed by a long disquisition on the law of comparative advantage. Second, updating your irrational beliefs carries high costs and low benefits. Learning economics is pretty hard, and the better vote you cast when you go into the voting booth armed with your new understanding of the economics of international trade isn't likely to actually change anything. As much as I would like to think we all have the moral fiber necessary to help us overcome overwhelming incentives, it simply isn't a very good description of the world we live in.

Tariffs make us worse off, but they are relatively easy to implement and hard to repeal because of the incentives inherent in the political system. Understanding a problem is the first step toward fixing it, however, and maybe we should be hopeful, if not necessarily optimistic, that public understanding of economics will someday advance to the point that tariffs are just a little bit lower than they are now. As it has been said, if the result of all the efforts of all the economists over all of history results in tariffs that are one percentage point lower than they would otherwise be, we will have earned our keep.

## 31

# Force Strangers To Use Monopolized Schools

Education reform is a perennial hot-button issue, with teachers' unions like the American Federation of Teachers and the National Education Association spending vast sums to elect their preferred candidates and lobby them for reforms they find favorable. Interest in free market alternatives to government education has increased since the middle of the 1950s, when Milton Friedman tried to resolve the tension between schooling's possible spillover benefits (which provide a plausible case for government involvement) and government inefficiency.

Friedman and many others noted that while the presence of spillover benefits might be an argument for government subsidy, it is not by itself an argument for government provision. He argued in favor of education vouchers whereby the government would provide funding but a competitive marketplace would actually provide the schooling. School choice has a lot of prominent academic proponents (most notable

---

Carden, Art. 2019. "The Struggle to Get Education Away from the State." American Institute for Economic Research. November 13.

among them, perhaps, is Stanford University's Caroline Hoxby, who I will note is curiously absent from this volume), but it has faced fierce opposition from teachers' unions and others who deride it as a thinly veiled effort to redirect government money into private, religious, or corporate pockets at best or as an effort to covertly re-segregate schools using the language of free markets and individual liberty.

In *Education in the Marketplace: An Intellectual History of Pro-Market Libertarian Visions for Education in Twentieth Century America,* Kevin Currie-Knight of East Carolina University takes us on a guided tour of free market ideas about education as explained in the 20th century by Albert Jay Nock, Frank Chodorov, Ayn Rand, Murray Rothbard, Milton and Rose Friedman, Myron Lieberman (where he locates a distinct public choice approach), and others. He closes by pitting former school-choice proponent Diane Ravitch's proposals for reform against Ron Paul's.

*Education in the Marketplace* arrives at a very interesting time and complements two other books that have appeared since the beginning of 2018 that question the romantic view of schooling: Bryan Caplan's *The Case Against Education: Why the Education System Is a Waste of Time and Money* and Jason Brennan and Phil Magness's *Cracks in the Ivory Tower: The Moral Mess of Higher Education.* Both ask that we consider education as it actually *is* and as it *actually* performs according to the best data we have. Instead, we indulge romantic and unlikely visions about what education could be in the best world we can imagine and then say, when things don't turn out that way, that we're just not doing enough of it or just doing it the wrong way.

What is it, though, about classical liberal ideas that makes them worthy of a separate treatment with respect to education? Citing Brennan, Currie-Knight explains how the libertarian ideal is a society built on *consent* (p. 3). To this end, he chronicles a series of radical visions for education that diverge sharply from the mainstream understanding of schooling as something governments do in order to make us smart, holy, virtuous, or just civic-minded. He begins with Albert Jay Nock, who was against state schooling but who worried that if left wholly to their own devices people would choose to learn the wrong things.

As the father of three children who make questionable choices about how they spend their time and the media they consume, I have a certain degree of sympathy for Nock's point and will note that a lot of our cultural output (and many of our educational institutions) are sponsored by states or by philanthropists who, presumably, want to see us make good choices with respect to the cultural and moral choices we make. And "by *culture*, Nock meant 'knowledge of the best that has been thought and said in the world'" (quoted on page 27). A cursory glance at the prime-time TV listings should be enough to convince us that the best people have said, written, and thought is not at the top of our priority list.

Here, though, we run into knotty questions about cultural preservation. Who, I wonder, should we trust to steward culture? Incidentally, Currie-Knight's project is made much easier by the (private) efforts of organizations like the Liberty Fund, the Foundation for Economic Education, and the Ludwig von Mises Institute—organizations that have devoted considerable resources to publishing programs making it easy for anyone with an internet connection to find the finest that has been written in the classical liberal tradition.

He begins with Albert Jay Nock on the basis of what he admits (p. 10) was an error: after seeing how Nock defended markets and criticized government education, Currie-Knight simply *assumed*…that his solution to the ills of state education would be markets in education. Further research revealed Nock to be as much a skeptic of markets in education as a critic of state education. Yet this itself makes for an interesting reason to start a project like this with an exploration of Albert Jay Nock. Particularly as Nock's libertarian thought was such an influence on Frank Chodorov—the second intellectual I examine—there is an interesting story to tell about why, for all his libertarianism, Nock did not support markets in education the same way as in other areas, while Chodorov did. (pp. 10-11)

Nock's importance in part came from his influence on Chodorov. He was a pessimist, in short, about markets providing the right education, arguing that what people want is not necessarily what they *should* want and what they *would* want if they know what is good for them (p. 23). How is Nock weighing the differences between the for-profit and non-profit sectors in providing schooling?

Currie-Knight points out that Nock was "influenced heavily by philosopher Herbert Spencer" (p. 25). Spencer is, of course, notorious (albeit unfairly) on the left for "social Darwinism." To what extent did Spencer's vision here influence Nock's ideas about schooling? On page 42, he points out that Nock was "deeply influenced" by Henry George. How so, and how did this manifest itself in the works of Nock and Chodorov specifically? Frank Chodorov agreed with Nock about the need for schooling as a means of preserving civilization, but he trusted parents more than he trusted the state "because parents had more vested interest in ensuring their children received quality education" (p. 57; Currie-Knight's words).

The move for government schooling was driven in no small part by an unhealthy dose of anti-Catholic bias (p. 46). This was, of course, a problem, and it was one Frank Chodorov pointed out: it might take some time to develop a system where there are enough schools cheap enough for everyone. As Pauline Dixon and other researchers with the E.G. West Centre at the University of Newcastle point out, though, this is a problem that the world's poorest are solving by developing their own low-cost private schools (readers surprised that West does not get his own chapter would do well to remember that Currie-Knight's subject is *American* libertarians—he gets his due especially on pp. 112 ff).

Our understanding of schooling is incomplete insofar as we usually consider it an unalloyed good. A comparative-institutional approach to schooling and the analysis thereof would at least take into consideration the possibility that schooling provides public *bads*, as well, insofar as schools indoctrinate students into well-intentioned but tragically misled ideologies. There is, of course, a devil in the institutional details, as well: who gets to define exactly what we mean by *education*? It is more than an effort to dodge a difficult question. Ideally, when we talk about "education" we are actually talking about something that can, at least in principle, be measured and defined objectively. This leads us, I think, to an underappreciated aspect of school choice and competition: "education" is defined in the process of its emergence.

The most controversial name in the book (due to name recognition) is Milton Friedman, the late-20th-century lion of libertarian ideas who proposed education vouchers in the mid-1950s. To Friedman, government's role in schooling came from funding by redistribution, not from administration (cf. pp. 11-12). As Currie-Knight points out (pp. 108-9), Friedman was basically asking for a GI Bill for K-12 education. Educational choice at the college level has helped produce in the United States the world's foremost system of higher education. The same, perhaps, could happen at the K-12 level.

As with virtually everything else, Friedman was not asking, "What is ideal?" Rather, he was asking, "What is the most prudent course of action that will lead us to at least a marginally better outcome?" Friedman is an exemplar of what Thomas Sowell called *The Constrained Vision*. He has taken a lot of fire for his voucher proposal and his grudging admission that in the short run, segregationists might use them to keep schools segregated. He believed, however, that in the long run school choice would lead to greater integration, and there is at least some evidence from studies of Virginia's tuition-grant program that some parents were using the grants to send their children to integrated schools.

School choice was not, as it happens, invented out of whole cloth by people seeking to maintain segregation in the wake of the *Brown vs. Board of Education* decision. Indeed, they go back to John Stuart Mill (pp. 106-7).

A close second for "most controversial name in the book" would be Ayn Rand. Rand and Isabel Paterson—and *Education in the Marketplac*[23] is a useful introduction to them and their characters—were very skeptical of government schooling. Rand distrusted it because of homogenization (p. 62); *The God of the Machine* author Paterson agreed with Rand that students were being taught collectivism in public schools (pp. 66-67, referencing specific progressive proposals). As Currie-Knight argues, progressive educators of the time saw the schools as vehicles for social change. To Rand, tax-financed schools were out of the question because they forced people to subsidize others and to support schools they didn't wish to support.

One of the major libertarian criticisms of government schooling comes from concern over what schools teach. Murray Rothbard, a brilliant writer, asked a penetrating question: what if we had a government-controlled press the way we have government-controlled education? Most of us would recoil at the idea and would be loath to move in that direction. At the same time, however, it seems reasonable to think that if we had state-controlled media, people would ask the same questions and have the same fears about a privatization scheme. Who will ensure that the poor have access to news? Who will ensure that the news is "fair and balanced"? I am not so sure I trust the men and women of the *educational* system, to borrow Adam Smith's phrase, to do it for me (cf. Currie-Knight, pp. 110-11).

*What*, we might ask, *about people who will fail to choose well?* It's certainly a legitimate concern, and one worth taking very seriously. However, a quick look over any set of local library shelves does not exactly inspire in me a lot of confidence that intellectual, moral, and cultural surrogates will choose wisely on my behalf. We have to take seriously the idea that schooling (as distinct from education) subsidizes a lot of public bads. I'm prepared to believe that preserving the greatest that people have thought and written and making it available for everybody is a very good idea. I am a lot less prepared to put cartoon strips, bodice-rippers, and new age pseudoscience in that category—and there is plenty of that on the shelves of the libraries we patronize.

While Currie-Knight is explicitly focused on 20th-century thinkers, I think the reader would benefit from a clearer and more complete connection between his subjects and their forerunners like Henry George, Herbert Spencer, John Stuart Mill, and Thomas Paine. What were the specifics of the influence, and to what extent did critics raise objections? A lot of people recoil from mentions of Spencer as a "social Darwinist"; might his influence taint (for example) the beliefs of Albert Jay Nock and Frank Chodorov? Moving into early 21st-century scholarship, what is it about schooling that makes people—even economists who believe the evidence points in the direction of vouchers—embrace it so, as Daniel Klein discussed in his 2005 paper "The People's Romance"?

In all, *Education in the Marketplace* is a valuable contribution to our understanding of how classical liberals think and have thought about schooling. Most people simply take it for granted that the state should own the means of educational production and glory in the collective action underlying that arrangement precisely *because* it is collective. There are a lot of ways this can be extended—by diving in to Diane Ravitch's conversion from school-choice advocate to school-choice critic, for example.

Intellectual historians and education historians might be disappointed by the lack of archival digging, but I suspect that more than one person will see in *Education in the Marketplace* a fertile source of new research ideas that take advantage of what might be found among the papers of Milton Friedman, Ayn Rand, and others. A classical liberal vision for education—and *Education in the Marketplace* is part of the Palgrave Studies in Classical Liberalism series—is a refreshing departure from the norm, and it is clearly something that needs to be taken more seriously in the coming years.

# 32

# Assume A Stranger With a Plan Can Run Other Strangers' Lives: Pandemics and the Great Mind Fallacy

"Surely," you might have heard someone say, "free markets are great at providing things like beans, cars, and Hollywood blockbusters, but surely, there are some things that are *just too important to be left to the market*." A quick Google search for the phrase "too important to be left to the market" gives us child-rearing, the environment, health, television, energy, education, housing, social media, "libraries' missions," finance, sports and leisure, food production, and water as examples of things that the invisible hand simply cannot handle adequately.

Markets are, of course, "imperfect" insofar as they cannot and will not produce utopia. It is a huge leap, though, from the sometimes-fumbling invisible hand to the idea that the visible fist of the state will make things better. A decade ago, the philosopher James Otteson built on the work of Adam Smith and Friedrich Hayek to explain what he calls

---

Carden, Art. 2020. "Pandemics and the Great Mind Fallacy." American Institute for Economic Research. April 17 "the Great Mind Fallacy." It helps us do the comparative-institutional exercise that, in turn, helps us learn whether or not something being "too important to be left to the market" really makes sense. As the political scientist and anthropologist James C. Scott argues, states excel at making the societies they govern legible. This is manifestly not the same thing as actually solving social problems. Combined, these help us see how, as the economist and Nobel laureate James M. Buchanan, "Order (is) Defined in the Process of its Emergence."

By now, it is cliched to reply that if things like education, finance, sports and leisure, and so on are really fundamental to human flourishing, they are too important *not* to be "left to the market." This isn't just a flippant, offhand expression of reactionary, ideological distrust in public institutions. It's a statement of deep conviction about the fundamental importance of market processes that harness and deploy the contents and convictions that inhabit billions of minds and that produce not the beautiful, articulated plan of a single Great Mind but what the philosopher, physician, and polymath Raymond Tallis has called "a boundless, infinitely elaborated community of minds that has been forged out of a trillion cognitive handshakes over hundreds of thousands of years."

States do not deal well with communities of minds forged out of cognitive handshakes. Scott has written a trio of books that underscore the point: *Seeing Like a State* (1998), *The Art of Not Being Governed* (2009), and *Against the Grain: A Deep History of the Earliest States* (2017). A 2010 Cato Unbound symposium[24] summarized his argument (note that these are not Scott's words, but those of the symposium editor): "...States can only exercise their power on what they can know about. Knowing requires measuring, systematizing, and simplifying." Measuring, systematizing, and simplifying don't sound so bad. They are, after all, what scientists and scholars do *all the time*. Here's the catch, though: "It requires, in other words, missing out on a lot of particular local data."

States are very good at identifying a well-defined problem and rendering a system *legible* to its functionaries. This is not the same thing as identifying the right problem (or set of problems) and providing anything approximating the "right" solutions. It is just finding something for powerful people to measure and control. In the process of making things legible, states give short shrift to other problems that are extremely important but that are outside the scope of their interest. If the goal is "stop the spread of COVID-19 at all costs," then an authoritarian lockdown seems like a pretty obvious solution. Once you relax the "at all costs" part of the goal, things become much less clear.

At a fundamental level, it looks like the theorists and practitioners who have slammed on the brakes of the free society are committing what the philosopher James Otteson (2010) called "the Great Mind Fallacy" in a 2010 paper in the journal *Social Philosophy and Policy*. He defines two problems, the Herding Cats Problem and the Gathering Information Problem, that plague any plan for state action. As he describes "the Herding Cats Problem of state action:"

"…because human beings have their own ideas about what to do, a legislator wishing for them to conform to his comprehensive plan, however beautiful and attractive in itself, is bound to be frustrated. Human beings upset patterns, as Robert Nozick said, and they do so in numerous and unpredictable ways. Hence, the legislator is faced with either giving up on his beautiful plan or attempting to impose it by force." p. 276

In addition to the problem of mutually-incompatible goals, he describes the Gathering Information Problem:

"The economist Friedrich Hayek argued that information about individuals, about their local situations, and about their personal goals, circumstances, opportunities, values is dispersed in concrete packages in billions of brains. For the legislator to devise a plan for society encouraging behavior that would lead to beneficial consequences, he would have to possess this information. But because this is impossible, Hayek argued, the legislator's plan, whatever it is, will be unable to exploit individuals' unique reservoirs of information, and thus the plan will be underinformed and overly simplistic." (pp. 276-77)

He combines the Herding Cats Problem and the Gathering Information Problem to give us the Great Mind Fallacy, which "is the endorsement of political and economic principles that require, to fulfill their promise, some person with the ability to overcome the [Herding Cats Problem] and the [Gathering Information Problem]." (p. 277)

COVID-19 policy, to say nothing of public policy analysis very generally, seems awash in the Great Mind Fallacy. Economists and other social scientists, for example, are under constant pressure to identify "policy implications" of their research, and I get the sense from my reading of the academic literature that a lot of us seem to think we are providing the arguments and parameters that a Great Mind will combine into an effective plan. Assuming a benevolent central planner might sometimes be a useful mental exercise or modeling convention, but it is something else entirely to think that actually-existing political institutions approximate these gods.

My friend and mentor David R. Henderson explored this in his 2020 AIER article "Liberation from Lockdown Now." As he puts it, some ten percent of the labor force has applied for unemployment benefits "because state governments are forcefully preventing them from working." Data on jobless claims illustrate the magnitude of the problem. There might be a strong argument to be made for increased liquidity in order to help people with sudden, short-term cash flow problems, but as Henderson notes, it is misleading to call the round of checks coming from the treasury a "stimulus" because "A government cannot stimulate production that it has forbidden."

Henderson asks: "Could the power of citizens' imaginations be unleashed to produce sufficiently effective social distancing at lower costs than what governments mandate?" We will never know, but he points to societies that have maintained open societies while keeping the virus in check. There is, of course, also the possibility that this will serve as a proof-of-concept for the next round of awesomely authoritarian interventions that government officials dream up. That's how Franklin Delano Roosevelt's Brain Trust saw World War I's War Industries Board, and as the economic historian Robert Higgs explained in his 1987 book *Crisis and Leviathan*, government power grew after World War I, after the Great Depression, and after World War II. It will, no doubt, grow as a result of the COVID-19 pandemic.

"But how will 'the market' handle the problem?" This is usually where a lot of people stop listening to economists because we can identify broad outlines and social processes, but it's rare that we can articulate and explain in minute detail *precisely* what the "solution" will be. We can't do this because we cannot articulate every aspect of every cognitive handshake out of which Tallis's "community of minds" has been forged. It is precisely the fact that people cannot specify in advance precisely how 'the market' will address the problem that makes markets indispensable. "The market" is not simply one technology among many for solving a well-defined problem. Rather, the market—shorthand for a system in which people are voluntarily trading private property and free labor—is a context in which the very problems we need to solve emerge and are defined. Or, to use the words of James M. Buchanan in his short but powerful essay "Order Defined in the Process of its Emergence,"

> "...the 'order' of the market emerges *only* from the *process* of voluntary exchange among the participating individuals. The "order" is, itself, defined as the outcome of the *process* that

generates it. The 'it,' the allocation-distribution result, does not, and cannot, exist independently of the trading process. Absent this process, there is and can be no 'order.'"

He continues a little further down:

"Individuals do not act so as to maximize utilities described in *independently existing functions*. They confront genuine choices, and the sequence of decisions taken may be conceptualized, *ex post* (after the choices), in terms of "as if" functions that are maximized. But these "as if" functions are, themselves, generated in the choosing process, not separately from such process. If viewed in this perspective, there is no means by which even the most idealized omniscient designer could duplicate the results of voluntary interchange. The potential participants *do not know until they enter the process* what their own choices will be. From this it follows that it is *logically impossible* for an omniscient designer to know…"

And then he gets to the heart of the problem:

"…unless, of course, we are to preclude individual freedom of will."

That is precisely what the interventions giving us what Gene Epstein has called "the Great Suppression" have done. A lot of people, of course, have no problem with that: there are more than a few iron fists concealed beneath health professionals' latex gloves. Forsaking the market, though, is a serious mistake because markets generate information and knowledge you simply aren't going to get anywhere else or, importantly, any other way.

## 33

# Say "Necessities Are Too Important To Be Left To The Market" During a Crisis

You've seen the pictures on your social media feeds: Empty shelves across America. Panic-buying. Hoarding. You might have even seen comments from self-described socialists saying, "Here's what the US looks like under capitalism in a crisis" and perhaps mocking people who point to regularly empty store shelves in Venezuela as a condemnation of socialism. There are two problems with this, though. First, this is a temporary phenomenon brought on by a sudden panic. Shelves emptied by panic buyers are rare in free market economies and frequent in alleged workers' paradises.

Second, and importantly, this is *exactly what the supply-and-demand model we teach in introductory economics courses predicts when we actively prevent the free market from functioning.* The shelves aren't empty because of free market capitalism. They're empty because of active interference

---

Carden, Art. 2020. "Those Shelves Wouldn't Be Empty If We Hadn't Stopped 'Capitalism'." American Institute for Economic Research. March 15.

with free market capitalism. Specifically, governments aren't letting prices change to reflect new market conditions.

States are declaring states of emergency, perhaps rightly so in light of some of the risks we likely face as COVID-19 spreads. Bundled with sensible emergency measures like recommendations about social distancing, touching others, and so on are price controls as politicians rattle their sabers about "price gouging" and "profiteering."

These are basically embargoes on knowledge. Higher prices serve a crucial social role by asking people to think a little harder about whether or not they really *need* that much hand sanitizer or toilet paper or whether they might be able to get by with a little less. The unintended consequence? There's a roll of toilet paper or a bottle of hand sanitizer waiting for the next person who wants it at the market price.

This gets turned upside-down when we go after so-called "price gougers." Grotesquely, they get tarred as villains while it's actually the politicians who are making the problem worse by interfering with prices. They are outraged that prices are rising in the face of high demand and uncertain future supply, but that's exactly what prices should do under these circumstances.

A lot of this stems from a fundamental confusion about *cost*. Critics and activists think that someone is selling unacceptably "above cost" and reaping an illegitimate windfall profit when they charge a price that is a lot higher than what they paid for the product from a wholesaler plus a "reasonable" profit.

This gets cost all wrong, though. At the point of sale, the cost of selling a roll of toilet paper is not what the retailer paid the wholesaler. That's irrelevant to current market conditions. The cost of selling a roll of toilet paper *to you* is what the person behind you in line would have paid. Suppose you're willing to pay $2 while the person behind you is willing to pay $5. *Everyone* is going through a hard time right now; it's not exactly clear why the person behind the counter and the person behind you should give up their gains from trade for you.

At this point, people might be objecting, "But demand is a reflection of willingness *and ability to pay*, so it might be unfair to the poor." This makes intuitive sense, but I think there's a serious complication with the "ability to pay" qualification: namely, if you are fortunate enough to spend your last $2 on a roll of toilet paper for which the person behind you is willing to pay $5, then you are actually sacrificing not $2 for the roll of toilet paper, but $5. You're "paying," albeit implicitly, by *not* selling the toilet paper for $5—and you are, therefore, demonstrating an "ability to pay" of $5.

This is similar to an example I'm fond of using when I teach about opportunity costs. Think about tickets to sporting events. Suppose tickets to the Big Game are going for $500 each. By sheer luck, you find a ticket on the ground. Does this mean you now get to go to the game for "free?"

No. Going to the game still costs you $500 (plus the opportunity cost of your time). You *could* have sold the ticket for $500, but you chose to go to the game. Fundamentally, there's no difference between finding $500 on the ground and buying a ticket with it and finding a ticket on the ground that you could sell for $500. Hence, I'm skeptical of "ability to pay" as an objection to high prices during disasters unless transaction costs are really high—and even then, I think the solution is to identify and overcome the sources of the transaction costs.

But shouldn't people charge low prices because it's the *right* thing to do? Maybe. People respond to a complex mix of incentives and motivations, and one of the more heartening responses to the COVID-19 outbreak has been the way in which a lot of publishers have opened up their online products for students and instructors suddenly faced with moving their courses online. Benevolence is one motivation among many, though, and the fact remains that we get a lot more hand sanitizer, toilet paper, and other supplies when we make room for people who are just in it for the money.

You may not like their motivations, but they're doing something your state's governor and attorney general aren't doing. Namely, they're getting valuable emergency supplies into your hands. Maybe humanitarian impulses are elegant and more civilized ways of getting goods into the hands of the needy compared to the profit motive, just as a lightsaber might be an elegant and more civilized way of killing an enemy than a blaster. At the end of the day, though, both motivations (just like both weapons) get the job done.

As the economist Yoram Barzel explained in his under-appreciated paper "A Theory of Rationing by Waiting," it's hard to give away money in a way that actually helps the people we want to help. As economists point out whenever price ceilings come up, price ceilings don't reduce what we pay. They change *how* we pay, with more of the putative benefits of our purchases being consumed by search costs. Someone waiting in a long line for low-priced hand sanitizer and toilet paper is incurring a cost (his valuable time) but not producing a benefit for someone else.

Here's a real-life illustration. Various outlets report that a Tennessee man bought 17,700 bottles of hand sanitizer with a view toward selling them at a markup online. Amazon refuses to do business with him, which is their right as a private firm. However, they would probably expose themselves to multiple price-gouging prosecutions were they to allow him to sell hand sanitizer at a hefty markup via their site.

The perverse result is that instead of 17,700 bottles of hand sanitizer at a price of $10 or $20 or even $100, people can, at least in the very short run, get *no hand sanitizer at any price*. The effective price of a bottle of hand sanitizer when there is none to be had, as Michael Munger has pointed out, is effectively infinity.

## Say "Necessities Are Too Important To Be Left To The Market" During a Crisis

This is a difficult time for a lot of people, and it's understandable and admirably humane to want to help others in their time of need. We aren't doing them any favors, however, by saying that they won't be allowed to pay very much for a bottle of hand sanitizer they can't get anyway.

## 34

# Make It Illegal to Work For Under $15 An Hour

When 2018 turned into 2019, the minimum wage in New York rose to $15 per hour. Then the *New York Times* reported that "Fast Food Workers Now Battle Unfair Firings."[25] The *Times* discusses several examples of people who were dismissed for what look like small offenses. These firings aren't inexplicable or arbitrary. They are the predictable consequence of a binding minimum wage in a competitive labor market.

How? First, according to the very simple version of the labor market economists teach in introductory economics courses, a minimum wage raises the quantity supplied and reduces the quantity demanded. The minimum wage, therefore, reduces employment. It's a robust thesis with ample empirical support from (for example) University of California-Irvine economist David Neumark and Texas A&M University economist Jonathan Meer, both of whom are affiliated with the National Bureau of Economic Research.

---

Carden, Art. 2019. "Protip: If They're Working to Get You Fired, They're Not Your Friends." Forbes. February 15.

The firings documented by the *New York Times* illustrate another hidden cost of minimum wages that goes beyond the disemployment effect. Indeed, Meer and his coauthors have explored parts of this empirically: minimum wages change *how workers are compensated*. Even if no one is fired immediately, workers can still be made worse off.

Workers do not live on wages alone. Think of all the things that go into a job. There are fringe benefits, for example, like health coverage, stock purchase programs, and incentive pay. The AP reported in October 2018 that when Amazon loudly raised the minimum it would pay to $15, it more quietly cut a lot of other kinds of compensation.[26] Some jobs are fun and rewarding (like being an economics professor). Other jobs pay relatively little but offer great work-life balance and a lot of schedule flexibility. Low wage jobs—like some of the jobs I held as a teenager—offer a lot of opportunities to build skills and, in some cases, to make mistakes without consequences that are too dire.

A minimum wage, however, restricts the variety of arrangements to which employers and employees might agree. In a competitive market, requiring workers to take higher wages means getting rid of some of the other things that would have made the job attractive. These might include things like free meals and uniforms. It might also include flexibility with one's schedule and forgiveness when one has to miss a shift.

The *Times* reports on the case of Princess Wright, a student a few months from graduation, who was fired from a Brooklyn McDonald's where she has worked since 2014 after she missed a shift. According to the *Times*, "she had called several hours in advance of a scheduled shift to tell her boss that she was staying home to help her landlord out of a jam by babysitting." Her employer "cited some tardiness that she said resulted from conflicts with her classes at Mercy College" in her dismissal.

At lower wages, we would expect firms to be a little more forgiving. As a teenager in 1993, I earned $5 an hour. Adjusted for inflation using the Consumer Price Index, that was around $8.50 an hour in 2019. New York City's minimum wage was $13 an hour in 2018, and it rose to $15 an hour in 2019.[27] For $8.50 an hour, firms might be willing to put up with a bit of uncertainty as to whether a worker will *always* show up on time or *always* cover shifts. For $13 an hour—and now $15 an hour—it isn't that surprising that fast food restaurants prefer to dismiss people who ask for periodic scheduling accommodations. Or maybe they don't hire them in the first place and instead replace them with people who are willing to make sacrifices and endure all sorts of stress and inconvenience. This, incidentally, is exactly what the supply-and-demand model economists teach in introductory economics predicts.

As the economist David Henderson has put it, "(s)omeone who intentionally gets you fired is not your friend." While I very much doubt that a lot of minimum wage advocates wake up in the morning *intending* to get New York City fast food workers fired, her dismissal is a predictable consequence of the minimum wages and other regulations they advocate.

## 35

# Believe That Governments Are Magic

The coronavirus pandemic has all the earmarks of a classic market failure: with every action, you create benefits or costs that spill over onto other people. When you get a flu shot, you make it less likely that people will get the flu. When you wash your hands carefully, you make it less likely that you will pass on illnesses like COVID-19. The people who benefit from your attention to your health and hygiene, however, don't compensate you for your valuable service.

This means there is a discrepancy between the private and social benefits from flu shots and careful hand washing, and according to the standard stories about externalities that we teach in introductory economics classes, we probably won't do as much as would be socially optimal.

Not enough people get flu shots. Not enough people wash their hands carefully. As I wrote in summer 2020, "just because an externality exists doesn't mean the market has 'failed' enough for command-and-control

---

Carden, Art. 2020. "The Anatomy of Government Failure in a Pandemic." American Institute for Economic Research. March 25.

regulation or even corrective taxation to be appropriate." The stories we tell in introductory economics classes also tend to assume away the problem of *government failure*—and governments are failing mightily in response to the COVID-19 epidemic.

Consider just one example from the Food and Drug Administration. Before I proceed, I want to make something abundantly clear: I have no reason to think that the people who work for the FDA are anything other than fine, upstanding people who want nothing but what is best for the world. No doubt, many people working for the FDA are putting in a lot of extra hours in response to the pandemic.

And yet they are, on many margins, actively making things worse. Consider this headline: "San Francisco startups have suspended sales of some coronavirus test kits after the FDA issued a warning."[28] The FDA has issued new rules governing testing procedures and products, but as *Business Insider* notes, "The new guidelines aim to speed up the approval process for labs in the US making COVID-19 tests, but the rules have caused confusion."

For a country that lags behind the rest of the developed world in coronavirus testing, this is simply remarkable. If the FDA is staffed top-to-bottom by competent and compassionate people, why are they making policies and issuing rules that are actively making it *harder* for people to get tested?

The fault is not in their stars or in themselves, but in their incentives.

As rule-makers, FDA officials do what rule-makers do best and, importantly, what rule-makers are rewarded for: they make rules. They have strong incentives to create vivid and intuitive fixes for easy-to-understand problems. In the case of the at-home COVID-19 tests, the possibility of fraudulent test providers is a pretty easy-to-understand problem. "Stop everyone from testing until we've sorted out the unscrupulous" is a vivid and intuitive fix for the problem.

However, it's a "fix" that ignores the often-ingenious ways people solve problems in commercial societies. It's also a "fix" that denies people the right to make their own decisions about the risks they will bear. The world has gone into suspended animation in response to COVID-19; it seems unreasonable to throttle at-home testing—and in the process, likely make the problem worse—in order to prevent a few bad tests from getting through. If COVID-19 is the threat to global health everyone seems to think it is, then allowing and even encouraging at-home testing seems like it passes a cost-benefit test even if some people will peddle fraudulent tests.

Of course, if bad tests or bad drugs get through the screening process, then the regulators at the FDA would be blamed. There might be hearings. People might lose their jobs. Decent people at the FDA might hear "you could have prevented this" from other decent people suffering from loss and tragedy. No one wants that on their conscience—to say nothing of their resume.

What happens, though, when the FDA prevents a good test from getting through? People suffer and people might die, but the connection from the FDA's action—or lack thereof—and the result isn't quite as clear. Someone, somewhere would have gotten tested and gotten treatment earlier with an at-home COVID-19 test. Now they won't. That person will suffer needlessly. Maybe he or she will die and be every bit as dead as someone who dies because of a bad COVID-19 test.

The line connecting the FDA's (in)action and the tragedy will be a lot harder to see. When a bad test gets through and someone gets hurt, it's really easy to see the causal link between the FDA's approval of the bad test and tragedy. Newspapers can interview the victim or take pictures of the body. That someone has been harmed by a fraudulent test is crystal clear. When a good test doesn't get through, however, it will be harder to find someone to interview. There may not be a body a newspaper can photograph that can be connected with certainty to the FDA's mistake.

This means, ultimately, that regulators have incentives to be *too* cautious. They will likely face serious professional and personal consequences for making one kind of mistake (approving a bad drug), but they likely will not face serious professional and personal consequences for making another kind of mistake (failing to approve a good drug). They are quite literally being set up to fail.

Market failure is a real and important phenomenon that shouldn't be overlooked. We also shouldn't overlook government failure, as well. Importantly, we need to be very clear about the problems that create government failure.

It likely cannot be fixed by electing or appointing "better" people or by giving regulatory agencies like the FDA bigger budgets. Their failures are a product of their incentives, not their intentions—and until their incentives change, we can expect to see a recurring pattern of government failure.

*I first learned about this from Alex Tabarrok at MarginalRevolution.com. The Independent Institute, for whom I serve as a Research Fellow, maintains the very helpful website FDAReview.org.*

## 36

# Debauch the Currency: The Austrian Theory of the Business Cycle, in Brief

The price system is a thing of beauty. F.A. Hayek was exactly right when he said that it would be considered among humanity's greatest achievements had it actually been designed, created, and implemented. Instead, it just emerged without central planning or a wise order from a wise ruler.

The prices free markets generate aggregate and convey important information about what, how, where, when, and for whom to produce. As the economist Tim Harford put it in his book *The Undercover Economist*, competitive markets create a *world of truth*: he notes that in a competitive market, we produce the right stuff the right way for the right people and in the right proportions. The properties of competitive equilibrium have a certain beauty to them. We produce everything that is worth more than it costs to produce. We produce nothing that is

---

Carden, Art. 2020. "How Everyone Messes Up at Once: Austrian Business Cycle Theory, Summarized." American Institute for Economic Research. December 20.

worth less than it costs to produce. What gets produced is produced by the lowest-cost producers and consumed by the highest-value consumers. It's an undesigned and unappreciated marvel.

That raises an uncomfortable question. If markets are so great, why do we have business cycles? What's the deal with the roller coaster rides of boom and bust that create widespread reductions in output and employment, also known as recessions? If markets are so great, why do we have business cycles?

There are a lot of reasons.

In what follows, I want to explore one of the elements of the Austrian theory of the business cycle: a cluster of errors by people who, presumably, aren't stupid and who, presumably, don't waste resources intentionally. Here's the punchline: monetary mischief means that prices are conveying inaccurate information about what, when, where, how, and for whom to produce. The signals that make markets work—prices, profits, and losses—are distorted relative to those that would what would tell the truth about underlying patterns of preferences and production possibilities. Hence, people make systematic errors. The prices, in other words, are lying.

Friedrich Hayek emphasizes the price we pay for the right to use other people's money and stuff *now* rather than later: the interest rate. Let's consider a couple of concrete scenarios. In the first case, the interest rate changes due to a change in saving and tells us the truth about people's willingness to sacrifice present for future consumption. In the second case, the interest rate lies about what is really going on because the creation of new money is not the same thing as the creation of new resources. Here's a parable: the parable of the asteroid miners and the chicken restaurants.

Suppose there is a change in people's saving behavior. James M. Buchanan's *Ethics and Economic Progress* devotes one chapter to the idea that, by our own standards and preferences, we would be better off if we all saved more—hence, Buchanan argues, the saving ethic has important "economic content." Suppose that, on hearing this, people generally start saving more. This increases the supply of loanable funds and decreases the interest rate.

In his legendary lectures on Austrian business cycle theory, Roger Garrison distinguishes between the *derived-demand effect* and the *interest rate effect*. For retailers, restaurants, and other firms that serve consumers directly, the derived-demand effect dominates. If people suddenly stop buying sandwiches at Popeye's and Chick-fil-A, this is going to have a larger effect on their production decisions than lower borrowing costs.

In the late stages of production, firms like Popeye's and Chick-fil-A contract (relative to what they would have done, at any rate) because they aren't selling as many sandwiches. Their (relative) contraction is a big part of what frees up the resources that make it easier for firms farther removed from immediate consumption to expand—companies like asteroid-mining firms with their eyes on asteroids said to be worth billions or trillions or even quintillions of dollars.

These firms expand because the interest rate effect dominates the derived-demand effect. They are far enough removed from the retail market for chicken sandwiches that what's going on there isn't going to affect them much. What will matter will be what the falling interest rates tell them about the wisdom of long-term investment. Lower interest rates make far-future payoffs more valuable.

At an interest rate of 5 percent, $1,000 one year from today is worth $952.38. At an interest rate of 1 percent, it is worth $990.10. The interest rate is transmitting extremely valuable information: people are now more willing to wait than they were before. Hence, it is a better idea to invest in projects that aren't going to pay off for a very long time. Even if the payoff is a thousand years from now, we can in principle estimate the present value of a $700 quintillion asteroid. Suppose this is off by many orders of magnitude and the asteroid is worth "only" $7 quadrillion. If the interest rate is 1 percent and the payoff isn't coming for a thousand years, that $7 quadrillion asteroid still has a present value of over $334 billion. At an interest rate of 2 percent, it's about $17.5 million.

The interest rates are almost certainly too low because asteroid mining is a pretty risky venture. Lloyd's of London will insure a lot of things, but the possibility of a 70.25-mile-wide asteroid hitting the Earth is a pretty spectacular risk. The interest rates are low and the time scale is kind of absurd to make a point: small changes in interest rates can lead to big changes in asset values.

This all goes fine if the changes are happening because of an increase in saving. Some firms and sectors—those closest to consumers—contract. Other firms and sectors—those farthest from consumers—expand. The economy grows faster as we add capital goods.

Things go awry, however, when the change in the interest rate comes from the monetary authority messing around with things rather than a change in saving. A credit expansion, where the monetary authority creates new money, lowers interest rates and begins a cascade of errors because the lower interest rates are sending incorrect signals about what is most valuable where. The monetary authority creates more money; it does not, however, create more real resources to support expanded production.

The lower interest rate has two effects, one on consumers and the other on firms in the early stages of the structure of production like mining, where all the action aims at creating stuff and skills that are a few years away from being finished goods or services. People consume more because interest rates are lower and the reward for delaying gratification isn't what it used to be. In response to higher sales, firms in the late late stages (like retailers and restaurants) sell more and make plans to expand.

## Debauch the Currency: The Austrian Theory of the Business Cycle, in Brief

In the earlier stages, the interest rate effect dominates. Firms in these stages, like the companies eyeing what they think are trillion- and quadrillion-dollar asteroids elsewhere in the solar system, see the present value of possible long-term investments rise. They try, therefore, to expand as well. In the short run, everything looks great. People are consuming more. People are investing more. Unemployment is falling, wages are rising. The economy is *booming*.

There's just one problem: prices are lying. Specifically, the interest rate is lying, and as Hayek emphasizes, the lying prices sow the seeds of an eventual bust even though everything looks wonderful.

Everyone is trying to expand their operations because of the lower interest rate and higher spending on consumption goods; however, there simply isn't enough real saving to support *everyone's* plans at the same time. To be sure, there are more loanable funds, which gives every appearance of real saving; however, people aren't actually cutting back on consumption and leaving *real* materials like lumber, bricks, and nails for others.

Every chicken restaurant orders more chicken at the same time, driving up prices and encouraging their suppliers to expand. They all plan to build new restaurants while, at the same time, asteroid-mining firms are borrowing money and trying to expand. This increases the prices of lumber, land, construction materials, labor, and everything else, but again, the real saving isn't there to support it. People are making terrible choices and systematically *mal*investing capital goods not because they are stupid but because the prices are not reliable. Importantly, this is not a theory of *over*investment, where people invest too much. It is a theory of *mal*investment, where people invest in the wrong things.

They find this out when it turns out the prices they expected to remain stable start rising. This is just an unpleasant surprise for some people who may not enjoy as large a profit as they expected when they decided to expand their chicken restaurants and chicken farms and asteroid-mining concerns, but it is a catastrophe for others who were just on the margin of deciding to enter the market and who pulled the trigger once interest rates fell (in the early stages of production) or sales jumped up just a little bit (in the late stages of production).

This means there are half-built restaurants and half-built office towers that can't be completed without more lumber, concrete, window glass, and copper wiring—but there are not enough of these materials to go around. A lot of people have nowhere to turn but bankruptcy. The boom is over, and a bust—during which capital, land, and materials are liquidated and reallocated—is the inevitable consequence.

*I offered a similar explanation in an article for DepositAccounts.com several years ago that, as far as I can tell, is no longer available on the internet.*

## 37

# Throttle Housing Construction and Make It Illegal To Pay More Than a Given Price to Rent An Apartment

An image showing a group of "Starving Jobless Homeless" people huddled outdoors next to a "Fully Robotic Coffeeshop" made the internet rounds a few years ago. The coffee shop, CafeX, features "Coffee from the best local roasters crafted with precision using recipes designed by top baristas." It's an image of the coming techno-dystopia in which robots take our jobs and leave everyone who isn't a capital-owning plutocrat to starve in the streets, no?

No. There are other things at play here. One reply to the tweet tagged John Stossel and diagnosed the problem immediately: the minimum wage in San Francisco is $15 per hour. That is a wage at which, apparently, the people in the picture cannot be profitably employed and which induces firms to look harder for ways to do with capital what was formerly profitable to do with labor.

---

Carden, Art. 2020. "Coffee Robots are Not Causing Homeless People to Starve." American Institute for Economic Research. April 12.

## Labor and Capital

"But firms will want to innovate and adopt new technology no matter what," you say. Maybe: it depends on what the technological possibilities are. If labor is extremely abundant, then the low-cost, most efficient production method might be labor-intensive rather than capital-intensive.

Think about why so many people don't buy the absolute-best top-of-the-line computers or smartphones. You probably don't. Consider the Cray XT5m supercomputer system, which

"starts around $500,000, takes advantage of the hardware and software advances of the Cray XT5 supercomputer, the basis of the petascale system currently in use at the U.S. Department of Energy's Oak Ridge National Laboratory."[29]

That's a heck of a machine, and if you're doing particle physics, it's probably nice to have. If all you need to do is check your email and manage a few spreadsheets, then it's overkill. Just as you wouldn't expect a firm to buy a Cray XT5m for everyone in the office and just as you probably don't keep one in the sewing room from which to check email and play Minecraft, firms aren't going to go for hyper-tech when that tech is hyper-expensive.

Again, firms will choose the lowest-cost way to produce a good in the interest of maximizing profits. When we use legislation like minimum wages and workplace safety rules and other things to increase the price of labor relative to what would obtain in the free market, we nudge firms toward replacing people with machines—as CafeX does, replacing human baristas with mechanical ones.

That gives us the phenomenon in the picture: a mass of people who are either unemployed or who have given up on the labor market huddled outside a robotic coffee bar.

The same principles also explain why they are without housing. First, building new housing in San Francisco is notoriously difficult.

*Reason* discusses an amusing-if-it-weren't-so-tragic case in which the owner of a laundromat is being blocked[30] from turning it into an eight-story apartment complex because the laundromat is "historic."

Making it difficult for people to build new housing reduces the supply of housing, which drives up prices. It also changes the composition of housing: high regulatory costs that make it hard to build *any* kind of housing will induce substitution away from modest housing and toward luxury housing.

Economists call this the Alchian-Allen effect after the economists Armen Alchian and William Allen. Adding a fixed cost to two similar goods will induce substitution toward the higher-quality good because it changes the relative price of that good.

The average quality of oranges in Florida, for example, is *lower* than the average quality of oranges in Vancouver for this reason. Suppose good oranges have a price of a dollar and bad oranges have a price of 50 cents. This means good oranges cost two bad oranges; a bad orange costs half a good orange. If it costs 50 cents to ship an orange—any orange—from Florida to Vancouver, it changes the relative price. Good oranges are *relatively* cheaper: with a total cost of $1.50 including shipping compared to $1 for bad oranges, good oranges only cost 1.5 bad oranges. The relative price of bad oranges rises, from half a good orange to 2/3 of a good orange. (The numbers in this example are from an example in Steven Landsburg's textbook *Price Theory and Applications*.)

People substitute toward higher-quality oranges and away from lower-quality ones. Before you say, "Wouldn't people *always* buy the highest-quality oranges?," note that there is a price difference. Then look in your own fridge or on your own kitchen counter. You probably don't have the absolutely highest-quality produce imaginable on hand.

Now, replace good and bad oranges with luxury and modest apartments and replace the fixed cost of shipping with a fixed cost of building.

Costly regulations make all housing *absolutely* more expensive, but they make luxury housing *relatively* cheaper.

If you're still not convinced, think about hiring a babysitter for $40 and going on a date. Would you go to Taco Bell? Or would you go somewhere nicer? Adding the price of the babysitter means going to Taco Bell and spending $10 each would cost you $60. Or you could go to a very nice restaurant and spend $40 each for a total of $120.

Without the cost of the babysitter, a trip to the very nice restaurant costs you four trips to Taco Bell. But the trip to the very nice restaurant is cheaper in terms of forgone trips to Taco Bell once you add the cost of the babysitter, which will cost $40 no matter what you do.

As the San Francisco Tenants Union explains, "In San Francisco, most tenants are covered by rent control."[31] Rent control is a standard example in introductory economics classes of a policy that hurts the people we ostensibly want to help. The Swedish economist Assar Lindbeck has said that "in many cases rent control appears to be the most efficient technique presently known to destroy a city—except for bombing."[32]

By holding prices below what the market will bear, rent-control ordinances ensure housing shortages, where, at the controlled price, people want more housing than firms and landlords are willing to provide.

Furthermore, they find themselves in a cat-and-mouse game with regulators because landlords and tenants move toward competition on non-price margins. Quality, to use just one example, falls because of rent control and necessitates, in the eyes of many activists, even more regulation.

The additional regulation raises the cost of providing housing, which reduces the supply of housing, which puts pressure on prices, and thus leads to more and more calls for rent control. The outcome is grotesque: all the new construction is high-end luxury housing while the rent-controlled housing deteriorates more quickly.

## Throttle Housing Construction

Adam Smith famously wrote that "there is a great deal of ruin in a nation." Does the picture of a huddled mass of homeless people outside a robotic coffee shop suggest the ruins of late-stage capitalism? I think not. It represents instead the "great deal of ruin" policymakers create when they make policy as if the laws of supply and demand are optional.

## 38

# Coddle the American Mind

In 2015, Greg Lukianoff of the Foundation for Individual Rights in Education (FIRE) and Jonathan Haidt of New York University caused a sensation with their cover story in The Atlantic titled "The Coddling of the American Mind." Their article quickly became one of the most read and talked-about pieces in the venerable history of The Atlantic, and it formed the basis for their 2018 book of the same title.

Their title is a play on Allan Bloom's classic *The Closing of the American Mind*, and they offer their own unique twist on a venerable genre of exposés about Kids These Years. Censoriousness is nothing new, but they note that there is an important difference between previous generations and what they document: the students themselves, they argue, have turned against freedom of speech.

Importantly, the authors note, they have medicalized offense and effrontery, referring to ideas they find offensive as "violence" and claiming that universities should be spaces where people, and especially people of

---

Carden, Art. 2020. The Intellectual Harm of Safe Spaces. American Institute for Economic Research May 20.

marginalized identities, are "safe" from "trauma." Of course, we want universities and all public spaces to be safe. However, the "safety" that has come into vogue as iGen—those born after 1995 or thereabouts who have grown up with mobile devices and 24/7 access to the internet—has come to college has been defined in psychological and emotional rather than physical terms. The censorious students seek not only physical safety but also protection from ideas that might make them comfortable.

It is, as they note, an affront to the very telos of the university, which should ostensibly be the fearless pursuit of truth wherever it may lead and not the pursuit of intellectual and physical comfort. Further, they argue, parents and administrators operating with the best of intentions have harmed and are harming the members of iGen who are demanding refuge from ideas they don't like.

These protectors and *Kindly Inquisitors*, to use the title of Jonathan Rauch's 1993 book, are unintentionally harming the people they are trying to protect by doing exactly the opposite of what we would want them to do if the goal is to create resilient, functional adults. The policy of shielding people from challenges to their worldview and values is a recipe for creating a generation of depressed, anxious neurotics who lack the ability to confront and address meaningful challenges.

The book is brisk and exceptionally readable. Lukianoff and Haidt organize their argument around what they call Three Great Untruths. First, what doesn't kill me makes me weaker. Second, always trust your feelings. Third, "life is a battle between good people and evil people." The first Untruth encourages people to avoid intellectual, spiritual, and moral challenges. The second encourages people to rely on the least-reliable elements of our psyches. The third strips the world of nuance and turns everything into combat and conflict between the forces of righteousness (Us) and the forces of evil (Them).

Throughout their discussion of these untruths, they identify the psychologically unhealthy practices endemic to them. It is here that they get personal. Drawing on Lukianoff's experience battling clinical depression, they highlight the ways in which demands for "safety" and refusal to entertain the notion that others might possibly be arguing in good faith lead to psychological absurdities and pathologies.

Rather than seeing, say, an on-campus lecture by conservative firebrand Ben Shapiro as an opportunity to sharpen one's own mind or an invitation into discussion, those indulging the Great Untruths see Shapiro's very presence on campus as an existential threat. Throughout, those who would deny speakers like Shapiro a platform engage in catastrophizing, or focusing on the absolute worst that could happen.

It would be a mistake to think that this is a left-wing phenomenon, though this dominates the narrative. They document outrages against free speech at Middlebury College, where Political Science Professor Alison Stanger sustained a concussion during a violent response to a lecture by Charles Murray of the American Enterprise Institute, but they also note the important problem of epistemic closure on the right.

Left-wing violence has led to injury. Right- wing violence, as with the motorist who ran down activist Heather Heyer in Charlottesville, has led to deaths. Or consider a tweet by George Ciccariello-Maher of Drexel University saying "All I want for Christmas is White Genocide." Is he actually calling for genocide? Of course not: in this case, he is coopting the language of white nationalists who have referred in many places to the left's goal as "white genocide"—and who have responded violently.

Their accounts of the infamous temper tantrums aimed at Nicholas and Erika Christakis at Yale and Linda Spellman at Claremont McKenna College makes the reader wonder if reading comprehension skills are really so poor at elite colleges and universities. Administrators' reactions to threats against Bret Weinstein at Evergreen State College can only be described as studies in cowardice. It is as if administrators do not know what every parent of toddlers and small children knows implicitly: do not negotiate with terrorists. And to present unreasonable demands—that Weinstein be fired, for example—based on an inability or unwillingness to comprehend his message and in a manner inconsistent with the telos of the academic enterprise is not literal terrorism, obviously, but it is toddlerish. Colleges and universities do students no favors when they give in.

Edmund Burke wrote that "it is no excuse for presumptuous ignorance that it is directed by insolent passion." The campuses that worry Lukianoff and Haidt are those in which presumptuous ignorance is strength, to borrow from George Orwell, and insolent passion is what ultimately matters. But as Christina Hoff Summers told an audience at the University of Massachusetts when someone screamed "Stop talking to us like we're children," "Quit acting like a child." And, as they note in their discussion of the riots at the University of California, Berkeley that accompanied an appearance by right-wing provocateur Milo Yiannapolous, the message sent by a university that did not discipline any of the rioters was this: "Violence works."

At issue in some cases is the adoption of the language of trauma and safety and the conflation of metaphorical with actual violence. They offer numerous important examples like the harrowing Title IX investigation of Northwestern's Laura Kipnis and the claim that Rhodes College philosopher Rebecca Tuvel's paper on transracialism that appeared in the feminist philosophy journal Hypatia somehow enacted "violence" on different communities. After reading her paper and some of the reactions to it, it seems like an entire field has adopted presumptuous ignorance and insolent passion as methods of "discussion"—and I use the term very loosely.

This would be very depressing if they didn't offer at least some possible ways out. Fortunately, they do. There is a fundamentally positive message in their explanation of the ways in which children and students are anti-fragile, meaning that they have complex adaptive systems that get tougher when subjected to stress. The advice they offer at the end of the book will, if adopted, reverse at least some of the trend toward the medicalization of disagreement.

They quote Hanna Holborn Gray: "Education should not be intended to make people comfortable; it is meant to make them think." It's a legacy we should reclaim as careful thought has to precede effective action. "Burn it all down" might sound nice to the insolently passionate and presumptuously ignorant, but it is reasonable to expect that what rises from the ashes will be worse than what we are trying to replace.

So here's what they recommend. Instead of "common-enemy" identity politics emphasizing a zero-sum struggle between groups, they recommend the common humanity politics of (for example) Martin Luther King, Jr. and the civil rights leaders who made important strides in the 1950s and 1960s. They also recommend adopting the practices of Cognitive Behavioral Therapy to avoid having our rational faculties overridden by our emotions. If microaggression is traumatic, how much more traumatic will it be for people to grasp that they have ruined lives and careers with their intemperate outbursts?

Lukianoff and Haidt ask, bracingly:

"What happens when you train students to see others—and themselves—as members of distinct groups defined by race, gender, and other socially significant factors, and you tell them that those groups are eternally engaged in a zero-sum conflict over status and resources?"

The answer is "nothing good."

Disinvitations and the like are discouraging but thankfully rare. There are thousands of colleges and universities in the United States that likely offer dozens of speaker events every week. The number of disinvitations is very small relative to the total number of events schools hold—but a high-profile disinvitation at a major college or university can have a chilling effect on the rest of discourse.

Colleges and universities (and, increasingly, high schools) are prescribing exactly the wrong kind of treatment for students confronted with ideas they don't like. They encourage people to avoid discomfort. To borrow a metaphor from Van Jones that Lukianoff and Haidt cite, they take the weights out of the gym and expect people to get stronger. Or, as CS Lewis puts it in *The Abolition of Man*, they castrate people and then bid them to be fruitful. *The Coddling of the American Mind* is an exhortation to stop and, thankfully, a guide to a better and more effective academy.

## 39

# Enslave People

In 1846, Karl Marx wrote the following to Pavel Vasilyevich Annenkov:

> "Direct slavery is as much the pivot upon which our present-day industrialism turns as are machinery, credit, etc. Without slavery there would be no cotton, without cotton there would be no modern industry. It is slavery which has given value to the colonies, it is the colonies which have created world trade, and world trade is the necessary condition for large-scale machine industry."[33]

Marx's claim reappears in a body of scholarship loosely called the "New History of Capitalism," which is a stream of books and articles that have appeared over the last decade or so. They are written mostly by historians, and they put slave-produced cotton at the center of the story of American economic growth. Books like Sven Beckert's *Empire*

---

Carden, Art. 2020. "Slavery Did Not Enrich Americans" American Institute for Economic Research. June 25.

*of Cotton*, Walter Johnson's *River of Dark Dreams*, and Edward Baptist's *The Half Has Never Been Told* tell vivid and moving stories about the obscene brutality of American chattel slavery, and they use words like "indispensable" to describe slave-grown cotton's role in American industrialization and modern prosperity. We are rich today, according to this line of reasoning, because of slavery. The cruel tyrant King Cotton, it seems, has returned to take his throne.

Economic historians have interrupted the coronation. The New History of Capitalism has come under withering criticism from economic historians like Stanley Engerman, Eric Hilt, Alan Olmstead and Paul Rhode, Robert Margo, and Gavin Wright. American economic progress, they argue, did not depend on slave-produced cotton. In a May 2020 paper in the *Economic History Review*, Wright responds to the central thesis of the New History of Capitalism by arguing that American slavery was a drag on the American economy, not a source of economic growth.

This might seem puzzling. The New Historians of Capitalism are keen to remind us that slave-produced cotton represented about half of American exports and was the leading commodity in Atlantic trade. In addition, they show in gruesome detail that there was blood on *everyone's* hands, from whip-wielding overseers to bankers approving loans collateralized with slaves. The leap from "slave-produced cotton was a big part of American exports" to "slave-produced cotton was 'indispensable' to American prosperity" runs into a lot of problems, though.

First, slave-produced cotton was a big part of a small sector. Compared to American exports, slave-produced cotton is huge. Compared to American output in its entirety, it's a lot less impressive. Make no mistake: the 5 or 6 percent of GDP cotton is a lot when you compare it to other sectors. It is not the difference between national prosperity and national poverty, however.

In *The Half Has Never Been Told,* Edward Baptist claims that "more than $600 million, or almost half of the economic activity in the United States in 1836, derived directly from cotton produced by the million odd slaves" (Baptist, p. 322). He gets this number by double- and triple-counting the same economic activity, by confusing stocks and flows, and as the economic historian Bradley Hansen argues in a devastating critique, "simply pulling numbers out of thin air, or a hat, or wherever it is that he gets them."[34] Stanley Engerman's description is apt:

"To go from a value of the Southern cotton crop in 1836 of 'about 5 percent of that entire gross domestic product,' to 'almost half of the economic activity in the United States in 1836' (pp. 321-22) requires his calculation to resemble the great effects claimed by an NFL club when trying to convince city taxpayers that they should provide the money to build a new stadium because of all the stadium's presumed primary and secondary effects." (Engerman, p. 641)

That's a degree of credibility we should all work diligently to avoid. Baptist, like the subsidy-seeking owner of the local sports team, is essentially arguing that 2+2 actually equals 8 because of "secondary effects." 2=1+1, of course; therefore, 2+2=2+2+1+1+1+1=8. QED.

Second, just because something happened as it did doesn't mean it literally could not have happened any other way. That as a matter of historical fact a lot of capital was tied up in slave-produced cotton does not mean that the capital could not have been deployed elsewhere. Slavery, as Wright argues, was not essential for cotton cultivation the same way it might have been essential for Caribbean sugar cultivation. He explains:

"Early mainland cotton growers deployed slave labour, not because of its productivity or aptness for the new crop, but because they were already slave owners, searching for profitable alternatives to tobacco, indigo, and other declining crops. Slavery was, in effect, a 'pre-existing condition' for the nineteenth-century American South." (Wright, p. 354)

Slavery was not essential or "indispensable" for cotton cultivation, as the widespread cultivation of cotton around the world and as the recovery of the southern cotton economy in the late nineteenth century demonstrate. Slavery and cotton, according to Wright, were connected "through historical legacies rather than technological or economic imperatives" (Wright, p. 355).

It's also a mistake to think that just because textiles played a big role (compared to everything else) in industrialization that textiles *had* to play a big role in industrialization. Textiles can be made out of a lot of things, though Beckert notes that producing an equivalent amount of wool would have needed "about 1.6 times the surface area of today's European Union" for sheep grazing (Beckert, loc 206 of Kindle edition). That might have been impractical, but people can do a lot of things besides graze sheep, spin yarn, and make cloth. The historical pattern might have been different and the Cotton Bowl in Dallas might not be one of the "New Year's Six" college football bowl games, but a change in the composition of economic activity does not need to mean a change in the level of economic activity.

Think about the characters in *Star Wars* and the actors who almost played them. What if Luke Skywalker had been played by Kurt Russell? What if Al Pacino and Burt Reynolds hadn't turned down the role of Han Solo? What if Jodie Foster and not Carrie Fisher had been cast as Princess Leia? What if Darth Vader had been voiced by Orson Welles? The cultural patterns of the last few decades would have been different, obviously, but it's hardly clear that *Star Wars* wouldn't have become an iconic film franchise without Harrison Ford as Han Solo or James Earl

Jones as Darth Vader's voice. It's also not like *Star Wars* was the only thing in theaters or on TV in 1977. Maybe *Smokey and the Bandit*—which came in second at the box office in 1977—would have become an iconic franchise had *Star Wars* been canned halfway through production. Or maybe *Starship Invasions*. Or *Spider-Man*.

In other words, *Star Wars* still would have happened had Han Solo been played by Al Pacino or Burt Reynolds. The American economy would have grown had cotton—or something else—been cultivated by free labor rather than slave labor. The specific pattern of economic activity would be different, but it's hardly clear the level would be lower. If anything, it almost certainly would have been higher: as Gavin Wright and so many others explain—among them Robert Wright in his 2017 book *The Poverty of Slavery*—slavery is a millstone around the neck of an otherwise-free economy. It enriches some people, but more generally it spreads poverty rather than prosperity.

As with many history books, the contributions to the New History of Capitalism assemble an impressive catalog of facts, and the books are written in such a way as to really bring the human tragedy of chattel slavery to the forefront. The New History of Capitalism misfires badly, however, in its interpretation of these facts. Slavery was not necessary for cotton, and cotton was not necessary for industrialization. Had chattel slavery never taken hold in the United States, we would very likely be richer than we are today. The "slavery=>cotton=>industrialization=>modern prosperity" argument seems to condemn American capitalism, but it is wrong.

## 40

# How Visions Backed With Violence Make Things Worse

Bernie Sanders' campaign for the 2020 Democratic presidential nomination and its own internal "fight for $15" reminded me of a passage from the Bible, specifically from the (cryptic) parable of the unjust steward: "Whoever is faithful in a very little is faithful also in much, and whoever is dishonest in a very little is dishonest also in much" (Luke 16:10). I think we can apply some of the lessons from this passage to the bigger and broader questions about whether or not we should trust people touting Big Plans and Grand Visions—especially when those Big Plans and Grand Visions involve them and their friends telling other people what to do.

The struggle between labor and management does not exactly inspire my confidence that Sanders and others who "feel the Bern" can be trusted to manage large chunks of the economy. The Sanders campaign is staffed by people who are ideologically homogeneous.

---

Carden, Art. 2019. "The Trouble with Big Plans and Grand Visions." American Institute for Economic Research. August 3.

They share a common vision of what the world should look like and how the world actually works. Importantly, they share a common and well-defined goal—"get Bernie Sanders elected President"—with pretty well-defined sub-goals ("win primaries") and sub-sub-goals ("get more people to vote in the primaries") and sub-sub-sub-goals ("target ad buys to maximize exposure among undecided voters in the states for which our team is responsible").

If they can't be "faithful in very little"—if they can't successfully and flawlessly manage labor relations in a campaign where everyone has the same ideas and the same goals—then why should we expect them to be "faithful in much"? What will they do when tasked with a larger and far more complex context, like managing the education system or health care system (whether these should be "systems" at all is another topic entirely), where the goals aren't as clearly defined and people's tastes, talents, and ideas are far more diverse?

Bryan Caplan once wrote an excellent post for EconLog about "Socialists Without a Plan."[35] He explains how he might be able to understand how a general or another military commander might be an enthusiast for central planning. After all, their job is to make a master plan, see that it is carried out, and adjust on the fly after meeting the enemy. Socialism demands this kind of (literal) military precision, but Caplan notes that the socialists he knows aren't exactly logistics experts. They're more "free spirits," which makes him (and me) wonder exactly who they think will do the detailed planning in a socialist society.

Several years ago, the philosopher James Otteson identified what he called "the Great Mind fallacy" that the person Adam Smith called "the man of system" commits so frequently. The Great Mind Fallacy assumes that all the relevant knowledge can be gathered, stored, and processed somewhere—but as Otteson notes, if no such Great Mind exists, then we have to discard or revise any arguments that assume its existence. Otteson explains how this blows up the argument for socialism in his 2014 book *The End of Socialism*. The disconnect between what the Sanders campaign proposes for the US labor market and what the Sanders campaign is actually able to accomplish in its own labor relations provides a vivid illustration of Otteson's point.

Somehow, calling it democratic socialism and relying on democratic deliberation is supposed to save the socialist vision. Even here I think the argument is off base: as much as I'm an enthusiast for deliberation, this seems to assume that there are unique, correct answers to big social questions that can be discovered if we would all just sit down and talk about it. First, there isn't one right way—so not only is there no Great Mind, there is no Great Answer. Second, even the deliberative mechanism peopled by faulty humans works passably but poorly. I remember in graduate school chuckling at a not-irregular occurrence, which was seeing a room full of economists leave a seminar room where they had just talked about the intricate policy details and implications of this model or that new empirical finding and then struggle to decide on a place for lunch.

Here's another example illustrating some of the problems with socialism, democratic or otherwise. Vladimir Lenin thought economic calculation would be easy: all that would be required would be "the extraordinarily simple operations of watching, recording and issuing receipts, within the reach of anybody who can read and write and knows the first four rules of arithmetic."[36] One wonders if Lenin had ever been to a restaurant and then tried to split the check. On a lot of Fridays in graduate school, my friends and I would visit one of St. Louis's many excellent Chinese restaurants and then laugh about how funny it was that a group of people pursuing doctorates in economics and finance were having so much trouble splitting the bill. Sometimes it's easiest and fairest just to split the bill equally, but we've all been at a dinner in which someone at the table takes advantage of the situation and orders immoderately. If that happens among friends and acquaintances, how much more likely will it be among total strangers?

The labor problems facing the Sanders campaign should make us pause for just a second and ask what it says about our ability to deliberate over, form, and articulate a Glorious Plan that will cure people's ills, correct injustices, secure domestic tranquility, and so on. One might be tempted to reply that these are the normal, run-of-the-mill problems facing any firm, group, or organization; however, it's important to consider this carefully because most firms, groups, and organizations aren't trying to take control of big chunks of other people's lives. Do the socialists want to organize and deploy the entire country's labor force according to a vision in which everyone gets $15 an hour and great benefits? That sounds nice. Perhaps they should show us that they can organize and deploy their own little platoon of campaign workers according to that vision first.

# PART V

# Ordinary Business Makes a Difference

# 41

# Business is Public Service

If you study business or pursue a business career, you might be praised for your prudence. It's unlikely, however, that people will think you are doing something especially virtuous or praiseworthy, and indeed if you are *really* successful you might be expected to "give something back" either through philanthropy or by paying higher taxes—which suggests, of course, that you *took* something in the first place.

What if *business* is really virtuous, praiseworthy, and underappreciated? In B*ig Business: A Love Letter to an American Anti-Hero*, the economist, foodie, and polymath Tyler Cowen joins other scholars like Deirdre McCloskey (in her "Bourgeois Era" trilogy) and James Otteson (in *Honorable Business*) in suggesting that being in business is not just tolerable but praiseworthy. In a very learned book that is nonetheless accessible to the general reader, Cowen dissects the ways in which American business supposedly has a baleful influence on the world. On the contrary, he notes, "business at its best is a fundamentally ethical enterprise" (p. 15).

---

Carden, Art. 2019. "Almost Everything People Say about Big Business Is Wrong." American Institute for Economic Research. June 28.

*Big Business*[37] is a comparative exercise that should make a lot of critics question their assumptions, to coin a phrase. Cowen is under no illusion about the perfection of business or even businesspeople, but at every stage, he interrogates objections to and criticisms of Big Business and asks, "Compared to what?" Is business uniquely fraudulent? Compared to what? Does business corrupt people? Compared to what? Are CEOs overpaid? Compared to what? Does business have undue influence on Washington? *Compared to what?*

Big parts of the book are pretty straightforward myth-busting. No, businesses aren't especially fraudulent. CEOs aren't overpaid (this will undoubtedly raise the hackles of a lot of people concerned about inequality). Work isn't soul-crushing and exploitative. "Big Business" isn't monopolistic. "Big Tech" hasn't turned evil. Wall Street actually does create value. Capitol Hill and the White House aren't wholly owned subsidiaries of large corporations. What you know about business, in other words, just ain't so.

Make no mistake: businesses and businesspeople do a lot of very bad things, and Cowen is frank about this. A lot of things in the "supplements" aisle at your local grocery store are snake oil, and firms still sell (and people still buy) penis-enlargement products that don't work (p. 22). Contrary to what the commercial tells you, you aren't going to find love by drinking more of a particular soft drink or beer. However, he argues that they do not do these things because they are businesses and businesspeople *per se* but because they are human organizations run by human beings. People in business lie a lot, for example, because they are *people* and *people lie a lot*. As Cowen puts it (p. 13): "So many of the problems with business are in fact problems with us, and they reflect the underlying and fairly universal imperfections of human nature."

What of the alternative institutions and organizations that bind us together and to which we might look for salvation? It's hardly clear that they are any better. When compared to the actually existing political, cultural, social, and religious institutions and organizations we observe rather than the very best we can imagine, business comes out not only un-damned but looking positively praiseworthy. When you compare the honesty and integrity of business to government, religion, academia, media, entertainment, and the nonprofit sector, it actually comes out looking quite good. An old joke goes: "How can you tell when a politician is lying? His lips are moving." Sex-abuse scandals have rocked major religious organizations. Colleges and universities promise "transformative experiences" that are likely selection effects rather than treatment effects. The news media tends to blow things out of proportion. Hollywood is rife with #MeToo stories (so, for that matter, is the professoriate). The world is filled with nonprofits that seem to exist for no real purpose other than fundraising.

If anything, the evidence suggests that business moderates these impulses and markets actually make us *more* trusting, trustworthy, and pro-social (pp. 28ff.). To the extent that businesspeople do bad things, it is because they are business*people*, not *business*people. Or, as Cowen puts it (p. 23), "The propensity of business to commit fraud is essentially just an extension of the propensity of *people* to commit fraud."

Cowen next turns his attention to CEO pay and asks if the conventional wisdom about executive pay—that corporate-executive suites are Old Boys' Clubs where the unscrupulous squeeze unjust compensation packages out of their shareholders and workers—is correct. He argues that it isn't. According to Cowen, "The best model for understanding the growth of CEO pay is that of limited CEO talent in a world where business opportunities for the top firms are growing rapidly" (p. 43) And: "It's not a popular thing to say, but one reason CEO pay has gone up so much is that CEOs themselves really have upped their game relative to the performance of many other workers in the American economy" (p. 44). In the language of an introductory economics class, CEO pay is high because of very, *very* high demand and very, *very* low supply.

Executive "power" likely has a lot less to do with it than we might think in light of the relationship between CEO pay and firms' market capitalization and earnings (p. 44). Cowen makes another sure-to-be-unpopular assertion: CEOs might actually be *underpaid* relative to the value they create for their organizations:

> CEOs capture only about 68 to 73 percent of the value they bring to their firms. For purposes of comparison, one recent estimate suggests that workers in general are paid no more than 85 percent of their marginal product on average; that difference is attributed largely to costs of searching for workers and training them to become valuable contributors. (p. 55)

The phrase "no more than" is important here as it suggests an upper bound on worker compensation relative to marginal product (with a wedge coming from transaction and training costs), but this certainly suggests that top executives are anything but overpaid—nor do they have more "power" than other workers to extract resources from their employers. Even the despised "golden parachute" packages that seem to reward unsuccessful CEOs for lousy performance have at least a plausible explanation.

Golden Parachutes encourage CEOs to take bigger risks—which shareholders might want to encourage—and sometimes, simply paying a bad CEO to go away when things don't work out might be a lot easier and less destructive than trying to organize an ouster. Due to the limits of space and the kind of book *Big Business* is, Cowen has to paint with a broad brush that leaves out details and nuance, but at the very least he makes a pretty convincing case that CEO pay lines up reasonably well with and is explained by CEO performance.

We should also love Big Business more than we do, Cowen argues, because it gives us the opportunity to do productive work—a source of meaning, contentment, and happiness for a lot of people. Importantly, work isn't disappearing, and I wish Cowen had explored this in greater detail. John Maynard Keynes predicted that we would spend a lot less time working. In one sense, he was wrong: people still spend a lot of time on the job.

However, the nature of "work" has changed. In his 1999 presidential address to the American Economic Association, the economic historian Robert Fogel differentiated between *earnwork*—the work we do to sustain our most basic functions—and *volwork*, which is the work we do to acquire the things we want rather than the things we need. The latter is now the lion's share of the work we do, and importantly, to the extent that work provides us with a sense of meaning and accomplishment, places to socialize, and so on, the line between "labor" and "leisure" gets blurrier and blurrier.

One of the most interesting chapters in the book looks at Big Tech and asks if it has turned evil. While he pays appropriate attention to privacy issues—facial-recognition surveillance—he argues that Big Tech has been and still is largely a force for good.

I have done multiple web searches to verify things in the course of writing this review (the date of Fogel's 1999 AEA presidential address, for example). As I was reviewing my notes earlier today, I changed my default search engine from Google to Bing. This was trivially easy, and it would be trivially easy to switch from using Chrome to Firefox, Safari, or another browser. The ease of switching browsers or social networks suggests to me (and Cowen) that fears of tech "monopoly" are likely overblown.

Fears of a population manipulated by "fake news," Russian bots and covert influencers, and out-of-control tech giants are also overblown. First, fake news and falsified reports are trivial bits of what happens on Facebook, and if anything, the veracity of what you see on Facebook compares favorably to "plenty of misrepresentations on television, in tabloids, in forwarded emails, in dinner table conversations, and in personal gossip" (p. 112).

The thesis that social media *per se* divides us is also inconsistent with the observation that "the most politically polarized Americans are the elderly, the group least likely to be getting its reporting from social media and the most frequent watchers of cable television news" (pp. 112-13). Finally, "from [Cowen's] naive, long-term historical perspective, Facebook hasn't come anywhere near doing the damage that the printing press (and radio) did by helping communicate the ideas of fascism, Marxism, communism, and so on" (p. 113).

Cowen also dispenses with two other things a lot of people believe: the view that high finance is predatory rather than productive (it isn't predatory) and the view that business controls government and bends it to the will of unscrupulous executives represented by unscrupulous lobbyists (it doesn't). This isn't to say that there aren't a lot of problems and a lot of things to fix, and Cowen is clear about this.

For the most part, however, financial intermediation successfully moves resources from areas of lower to areas of higher yield and, in the process, makes possible a lot of creativity and innovation. The $3 billion corporations spend on D.C. lobbying looks like a lot of money, but it's small change compared to the $200 billion they spend on advertising (p. 171). If the search for special privilege were as lucrative as a lot of people think, firms would probably be spending a lot more on lobbying than they actually are (parenthetically, if it were so easy to manipulate people, they would probably spend a lot more on advertising, as well).

Cowen isn't telling a Panglossian tale about how literally nothing could be better than the world we inhabit. For example, he is skeptical of people's tendency to develop actual loyalty to firms, and he thinks that customer-loyalty programs might have some anti-competitive tendencies. For all its imperfections, however, American business does a pretty good job—a much better job, Cowen argues, than most people think, and I, for one, agree.

# 42

# Speculators are Unsung Heroes

What about the people who make their living in markets? For all the aspersions cast on them by politicians, commentators, and others, they are, in pursuing their own wellbeing, advancing others' wellbeing, as well. Indeed, I have an idea for a new hero for Phase 4 of the Marvel Cinematic Universe: the Speculator. Consider this scenario. A hurricane has decimated a city in Florida and left its residents without much drinkable water or gas. It has also leveled lots and lots of houses, businesses, and buildings, which means Floridians will need lumber, nails, and all sorts of other building materials that are now in very short supply. This sounds like a job for ... *the Speculator*!

She swoops into action and buys lumber, nails, water, and gas in places like Birmingham and Boston that haven't been hit by the hurricane and where prices are still low. She then hires people to get all the supplies from where they are relatively abundant—Birmingham and Boston, again—to where they are relatively scarce and where they

---

Carden, Art. 2019. "It's a Bird! It's a Plane! It's ... the Speculator!." American Institute for Economic Research. September 19.

can be sold for a higher price. After paying for all the supplies, renting trucks, paying drivers, and so on, she is left with a very handsome profit.

To most eyes, this reads like the self-interested profit-seeking of a supervillain, not the selfless endeavor of a superhero. The scenario above is silent on the Speculator's motives beyond "earn a profit," and it is entirely

possible that the Speculator lacks proper and appropriate *beneficence*. Maybe this means she is blameworthy in this respect. Identifying and measuring proper beneficence is hard, though, and it can't be compelled.

Adam Smith put it this way in *The Theory of Moral Sentiments*:

"Beneficence is always free, it cannot be extorted by force, the mere want of it exposes to no punishment; because the mere want of beneficence tends to do no real positive evil. It may disappoint of the good which might reasonably have been expected, and upon that account it may justly excite dislike and disapprobation: it cannot, however, provoke any resentment which mankind will go along with."

Might her very narrow focus "justly excite dislike and disapprobation"? Perhaps, but it's not punishable. The Speculator may not act from the most laudable of motives—and hence probably might not be the best candidate for superhero status—but she is doing *exactly what we would want a superhero to do in this situation*. Specifically, the Speculator is getting goods from where they are relatively abundant (and therefore not as valuable) to where they are relatively scarce (and therefore extremely valuable).

Consider another scenario: oil. You have heard, no doubt, that we are going to *run out of oil*. Is there any hope? Can we escape the calamity? Whatever might we hapless citizens do? Once again, this sounds like a job for ... *the Speculator!*

The Speculator reasons that a shrinking supply of oil coupled with rising demand as the world's population grows and gets richer means that oil prices in the future will likely rise. In anticipation of these higher future prices, she takes oil off the market today and stores it for the future, when prices are higher. A few decades from now, when prices are higher, she sells the oil she has stockpiled and once again pockets a very handsome profit.

Storing oil, of course, is pretty expensive, and maybe she doesn't want to do it. She can still act on her knowledge by buying futures contracts that allow her to take possession of oil at a future date. She could also buy options that would give her the right to buy oil at a future date at a predetermined price. In any of these cases, she would profit from her superior insight. She would also move oil from *when* it is relatively abundant (right now) to *when* it is relatively scarce (the future). Again, she may not act from the most admirable of motives, but she is doing exactly what we would want a superhero to do: get valuable resources from where they are abundant to where they are scarce.

In his Nobel Prize address, Vernon Smith pointed out that "markets economize on the need for virtue, but do not eliminate it." Virtue is necessary if we are going to have what James Otteson describes as "a just and humane society" in his book *Honorable Business*. When we leave prices free to change based on supply and demand, the Speculator can get rich by moving resources from where they are of low value to where they are of high value. Importantly, this frees up the time, energy, and attention of others—heroes or not—who can then concentrate on other things.

The Speculator, I contend, gets a raw deal in the court of public opinion. How she uses the profits from her ventures, whether in riotous living or perfect virtue, is beside the point. In a well-functioning market where people are guided by the profit motive, however, these examples show that you don't need to wear a cape—or even be a particularly nice person—to do something heroic.

## 43

# So is Wandering Oaken from the *Frozen* Movies

The 2019 release of Disney's *Frozen II* brought back a lot of very good memories from the last several years. As of this writing, my daughter is ten, which means I know pretty much every line to every song in Disney's runaway mega-hit *Frozen*. A few years ago, she was in her grandparents' living room with her step-cousin Anna. It was as if they looked at each other with an unspoken understanding:

> I see that you are a little girl. I too am a little girl. Let us lift our voices and sing the song of our people. *The snow glows white on the mountain tonight, not a footprint to be seen...*

In 2015, I took her to see Disney on Ice's production of *Frozen* and got to experience the wonder of hearing an arena filled with little girls singing along—and the wonder of spending a sum I don't want to admit

---

Carden, Art. 2019. "Wandering Oaken Should Be Your Favorite Frozen Character" American Institute for Economic Research. December 25.

on a stuffed Elsa doll and some lemonade. Most of the girls there were dressed as Anna or Elsa, as were (from what I can gather) most of the girls who went trick-or-treating that Halloween. Googling "Frozen cosplay" gives you image after image of Anna and Elsa with the occasional Kristoff, Olaf, or Hans.

If you're going to dress up as a character from *Frozen*, though, don't pick any of the major characters. I suggest dressing as Oaken, the proprietor of Wandering Oaken's Trading Post and Sauna (in the French version, it's Chez Oaken Commerce et Sauna). He's one of the best characters in the movie.

For most of history, people like Oaken who bought low and sold high were dishonored and disdained. That began to change in the 18th century, and the sympathetic treatment of Oaken in *Frozen* is an interesting illustration of the rise of economic liberty and social honor for inventors, merchants, and manufacturers that explains why almost all the production that has happened in human history has happened in the last couple of centuries.

He is only in *Frozen* for a few minutes and doesn't have much to do in *Frozen II*, but it's clear Oaken is an irrepressible optimist and a family man who views buying and selling as an honorable profession. In the first movie, Anna comes upon his establishment while traversing the frozen landscape to find her sister Elsa. She enters, and a smiling Oaken advises her of his "big summer blowout" sale with "half off swimming suits, clogs, and a sun balm of my own invention, ja?!"

Oaken is treated sympathetically. He tells a practically frozen Kristoff that the carrots, rope, and pickaxe he wants to buy "will be 40." Kristoff objects and offers 10, to which Oaken replies by explaining that the rope and pickaxe are from their "winter stock, where supply and demand have a big problem" (the sudden winter-in-July implies a big spike in demand with a lot of uncertainty about future supply). Kristoff replies with his own "supply and demand problem—I sell ice

## So is Wandering Oaken from the *Frozen* Movies

for a living." Oaken holds firm at 40, offering to throw in "a visit to Oaken's sauna," where his family is currently enjoying the heat. He still holds firm, noting that 10 will get Kristoff the carrots "and no more."

Kristoff rebuffs a prying Anna, saying, "Back up, while I deal with this crook here." Oaken, a mountain of a man, will not endure such an insult and throws Kristoff out on his face. He returns to Anna, tells her he is "sorry about this violence," and says, "I will add a quart of *lutefisk* so we have good feelings." The whole scene—just a few minutes long—depicts Oaken the trader as a good guy who isn't doing anything wrong by holding firm.

The *Frozen* franchise is going to be a gold mine for Disney for a very long time. This became even more evident for me in the checkout line at Target when I saw a kids' book about Oaken inventing The Great Ice Engine.

In the book, Oaken is *honorable* because he has invented a machine that raises the ice cutters' productivity.

Oaken *and* the ice cutters disappear, and the ice cutters miss a delivery. Someone suggests that Oaken has been kidnapped by the ice cutters because he has invented a machine that might take their jobs—but this possibility is dismissed out of hand. It is discovered that they have gone to the next town to visit a blacksmith so they can replace a gear and find ways to make the machine better. They have an innovation-and-ideas jamboree and return to the frozen lake with a better ice-cutting engine. At the end of the book—and this is important—they talk about how the ice-cutting engine doesn't render the ice cutters useless. Rather, it makes them *more productive*.

Disney isn't trying to teach a morality tale about the glories of bourgeois life, just as the scene at the end of the movie where a royal proclamation cuts off trade between Arendelle and ~~Weaseltown~~ Weselton isn't a hidden commentary on international trade (if anything, it might resemble the early modern law merchant, where the duke is cast out of the ring of honorable traders despite his noble rank because it is clear he's a scoundrel—and there's a sense in which my critique of the movie is all wet). It's a commentary on what's in the air, so to speak. Innovation raises productivity. Oaken was not trading deceitfully or doing anything wrong by asking a high price, and intemperate Kristoff was wrong to call him a crook. At the end of the movie, Anna doesn't *fall in love with and marry a prince*, riding off into the sunset forever. She falls in love with ... an ice cutter.

In a sense, *it's just a kids' movie* and in a sense, *it's just a kids' book aimed at capitalizing on the movie's roaring popularity*. I think the movie and the book are more than that. They are part of the Great Conversation in a commercial society, and the sympathetic treatment of a character like Oaken in English, en Francais, en Espanol, in Mandarin, and in a lot of other languages illustrates the point Deirdre McCloskey is making in her "Bourgeois Era" trilogy. Economic liberty and social honor for merchants and innovators (like Oaken) made the modern world.

## 44

# Support Your Local Banker

Bankers are economic vampires who take, take, *take*, and give nothing in return. Or at least that's the impression you might get from a lot of popular discussions. On closer examination, however, bankers are value creators in competitive markets for loanable funds.

It is important that bank customers and bankers themselves do not misunderstand their role. In what follows, I will abstract away from questions about sound money, hard money, risk management, and so on so that I can focus on exactly how bankers create value. Drawing on some of the key insights in Michael Munger's *Tomorrow 3.0*, I will explain how bankers and other financial intermediaries create value.

If you ask a lot of people what business bankers are in, you might hear that they are in the business of making loans. Or maybe they are in the business of building relationships. Both contain an element of truth, but they're incomplete. Banks, fundamentally, are in the business of reducing transaction costs.

---

Carden, Art. 2019. "How Do Bankers Create Value?" American Institute for Economic Research. March 26.

And what, you wonder, are transaction costs? The 1993 Nobel laureate Douglass C. North defined transaction costs in his Nobel Prize lecture as "the costs of specifying what is being exchanged and of enforcing the consequent agreements."

Munger emphasizes three attributes of transaction costs: *triangulation*, *transfer*, and *trust*. He defines *triangulation* as "information about identity and location, and agreeing on terms, including price." *Transfer* is "a way of transferring payment and goods that is immediate and as invisible as possible." *Trust* is "a way of outsourcing assurance of honesty and performance of the terms of the contract."

If you're a banker, you're actually in the business of reducing these costs. You create wealth when you're successful. In their textbook on managerial economics for MBA students, Luke Froeb and his coauthors define the "one lesson of business":

> The art of business consists of identifying assets in lower valued uses, and profitably moving them to higher valued uses.

Bankers who move assets—loanable funds—from lower-valued to higher-valued uses are creating value (hence "profitably"). They overcome the transaction costs that otherwise gum up the works and keep assets in low-value uses.

## 45

# Is Duke Dropout Zion Williamson Wasting His Life?

The *Onion* is hilarious, and it's one of the true literary gems of the internet age (though, in my humble and evangelical opinion, the *Babylon Bee* has eclipsed it in slugging percentage in the last couple of years). One of its more interesting recent entries carried the headline "Duke Anthropology Professor Devastated to Learn Promising Student Dropping Out."[38]

The anthropologist in the article, "Edwin Greeley," is perfect in his obliviousness to the world that once-in-a-generation basketball superstar—and, according to the article, anthropology prodigy—Zion Williamson faces, and he doesn't understand "why anyone so talented would [drop out of Duke]."

The answer, of course, is obvious: many, many millions of dollars await Williamson in the NBA.

---

Carden, Art. 2019. "This Duke Dropout Could Reinvigorate the Study of Anthropology." American Institute for Economic Research. April 30.

At *Forbes*, Adam Zagoria asked if Zion Williamson could earn $1 billion in his basketball career.[39] Even though the fictional Greeley is convinced that "a $30,000-per-year adjunct professorship was easily within reach for someone with [Williamson's] promise," the choice just doesn't seem that hard.

It's beautiful satire.

Hold on a minute, though. What if Williamson can have both? It turns out he can: Williamson can play basketball and advance the anthropological project through the power of specialization.

Let's suppose Williamson truly is an anthropology virtuoso, unmatched by anyone in his class, and a once-in-a-generation talent in anthropology just as he's a once-in-a-generation talent on the basketball court. It doesn't follow that he is wasting his talents by dropping out of Duke and playing basketball instead of staying at Duke, possibly earning a Ph.D. in anthropology, and embarking on a long research career.

Maybe he's without peers as an anthropology student, but relative to the rest of the world he has even more singular talents in basketball—talents that will probably earn him in endorsements alone enough to fund an entire world-class anthropology department. Had he eschewed basketball and chosen anthropology, he might have put himself in a position to write one or two seminal articles every year and a breakthrough book every few years after a decade or so of intense study.

By specializing in basketball, where he has a clear comparative advantage relative to virtually everyone else in the world, and using the proceeds to fund research and teaching, Zion Williamson can give the world more world-class basketball and more world-class anthropological inquiry.

Would it be a tragedy if Williamson were an anthropology virtuoso who, in dropping out of Duke and taking his talents to the NBA, eschewed a career of path-breaking, world-rocking anthropological scholarship? No. By following his heart—and his wallet—Zion Williamson puts himself in a position to create more on-court excitement and more off-court insight than he ever could have had he chosen to forsake basketball for the life of the mind.

So what should he do? I don't know. I'm not him, I don't know his preferences, and I don't know which trade-offs he is willing to make. Maybe he *is* secretly pining for a career as an anthropologist and trying to gin up the courage to walk away from basketball so he can embrace his true love.

Lots of academic economists could probably make more money working on Wall Street, and yet we eschew big paychecks for the job satisfaction that comes with academia. Even if he has a passion for anthropology, what we know about specialization and division of labor shows us that Williamson needn't feel like he is letting anyone down or forsaking anthropology by choosing basketball.

If my experience with colleges and universities is any indication, I suspect there are plenty of people in Duke's advancement office who would be more than happy to remind Williamson of that fact and help him match his newfound riches with his intellectual passions.

## 46

# Bounty Hunters and Privateers: The Lesson of *The Mandalorian*

I'm a giant Star Wars geek, and I tend to be very forgiving. Hence, I loved the first season of *The Mandalorian*, the first new series on the streaming service Disney+. For the uninitiated, the series is about a bounty hunter, a Mandalorian, who is just known as "Mando" and who makes his living by scooping up bail jumpers and other prizes.

The series has me thinking about private security, particularly as we get ever closer to the twentieth anniversary of the September 11, 2001 attacks and as we get to the point where more and more soldiers who go to Afghanistan will be going to fight a war that started before they were born.

Might *The Mandalorian* at least get us thinking about whether or not there are better ways to do this? Better ways to enforce the law? Better ways to deal with people who do terrible, horrible things? At the very least, might we get similar outcomes for a lower price?

---

Carden, Art. 2020. "Bounty Hunters and Privateers in The Mandalorian." American Institute for Economic Research. March 30.

I suspect we can. Even if we had put bounties of *billions* on the heads of Osama bin Laden and his henchmen, we likely could have gotten a similar result at a much lower cost than the *trillions* we have spent on war since 9/11/01. I suspect there would have been a lot less collateral damage. Indeed, Ron Paul proposed something like this after the 9/11 attacks.

It wouldn't be a radically new thing. Historically, countries would issue letters of marque and reprisal against pirates and enemy ships with payout going to whoever brought in the cargo. Privateers were basically bounty hunters.

In the first episode, we learn a lot about rules among the bounty hunters and specifically the treaties and agreements that govern bounties, their capture, and the distribution of the spoils. I'm reminded in reading all this of Peter Leeson's work on anarchy, pirates, and the constitution of piratical consent. Moreover, I'm reminded of Edward Stringham's work on the history of private security, a lot of which provides at least a proof of concept for the private provision of what is nominally a public good.

Consider the incentives facing the bounty hunter. Will they waste resources? It isn't likely. During one exchange about a possible bounty, Mando tells Carl Weathers that 5,000 "won't even pay for the fuel." He has an incentive to be a bit more careful about what he says "yes" and "no" to than someone who is spending other people's money. Contrast this with someone who is simply voting for or against war. They don't have any skin in the game, and therefore, they don't have an incentive to compare costs and benefits clearly and completely.

It's illustrated during a bit where the Mandalorian finds himself bargaining over stolen goods. The problem, and what makes it intriguing, is that he's trying to buy back stolen parts from his own ship (think about this the next time you hear about people seeking federal grants). There is an interesting Coasian experiment, and an interesting exercise for living, in the second episode (parenthetically, I'm pretty sure I understand the "no disintegrations" line in *The Empire Strikes Back*). Jawas strip Mando's ship of a lot of valuable parts—rendering it essentially unflyable—and Mando has to get his parts back. He fails to get his stuff back when he attacks the Jawas' land barge and ends up in a situation where he is protesting the injustice of having to buy back the parts the Jawas stole. Unjust? Undoubtedly, but, for the most part, irrelevant. The Mandalorian isn't in a situation to debate the injustice of his parts being stolen. He just needs them back. Hence, bargaining with the Jawas for the stolen merchandise is the best of his unlovely options.

I'm reminded of discussions I've had with Michael Munger and presentations he has given on institutions and how they evolve (a lot of this is similar to the work being done by Barry Weingast and his last decade or so of work with Douglass North and John Joseph Wallis). In some cases, injustice is just something we have to accept in an imperfect world. Actually getting to a better position is the constitutional/institutional problem. In this case, the Mandalorian had to grit his teeth and accept one evil in order to prevent a much larger one.

In a later episode, the Mandalorian finds himself contract-fighting on behalf of a group of krill farmers who find themselves facing regular raids from nearby bandits with an AT-ST. I'm reminded of one of the things that has kept people poor for almost all of history: raiding and fending off raids. A few minutes of the episode show people training for their battle with the raiders.

There are a couple of ways in which we see resources being wasted. First, there are the raiders themselves. They aren't actually doing anything productive. They're investing in transfers (it's like robbing a record store, or lobbying). During the training scene, we see the people of the village preparing to fight with the bandits. What are they doing while they are training? They are preparing to protect their property, but importantly, they aren't actually farming any krill or doing anything productive. The big question in political economy, I think, concerns how the institutions emerge and what they reward. It's one thing to *say* that people are better off when they trade rather than raid. It's something else entirely to get the institutions right.

*The Mandalorian* is fantastic fan service for people who love science fiction, westerns, and Star Wars specifically. I'm excited about the long term future of the Star Wars universe given that, in a world with Disney+, we can expect regular new entries in the Star Wars canon (apparently, there are plans for an Obi-Wan Kenobi series and another on Cassian Andor). As always, there are some interesting illustrations of basic economic ideas and some ideas that are at the cutting edge of research in the social sciences. As I say pretty regularly, *economics is everywhere*. Even on planets visited by science fiction bounty hunters.

## 47

# Free Markets can Still Get the Job Done

"If the government doesn't do [X], who will?" It's a good question, and it's a fair one. We rely on governments for a lot of things, like police and fire protection. One of the classic objections to libertarianism is "who would build the roads?" And of course, there's "what about the poor? Can we guarantee that people wouldn't slip through the cracks if we didn't have a large and robust welfare state?" Can we imagine a world in which the government wasn't in charge of fire protection? Police protection? Roads? Welfare? Yes, actually, we can—and we can look to history for examples of the market mechanism working well. Was it perfect? No, but as Deirdre McCloskey has pointed out, it's probably a mistake to turn an imagined best into the enemy of an actually pretty good. Here are some examples.

***Fire protection***. Fire protection looks like a classic case of spillover benefits. There are: if your house is burning, it raises the likelihood that

---

Carden, Art. 2020. "If the Government Doesn't Do It, Who Will?" American Institute for Economic Research. April 9.

my house burns, too. As a 2010 example in Tennessee shows,[40] however, fire protection can be a private good. If you don't pay your water or power bills, your water and power get shut off. If you don't pay your fire department bill, then perhaps you shouldn't be surprised when the firefighters don't respond while your house burns to the ground.

But what about densely-packed cities where a small conflagration can lead to a city-wide disaster, as has happened in places like Chicago and San Francisco. As Fred McChesney argues, however, municipal fire departments were basically takeovers of the private sector in order to create patronage jobs for political allies. Private, volunteer companies were getting the job done for the most part. Then political entrepreneurs noticed a way to obtain power and resources for themselves by taking over previously-private volunteer fire departments and creating reliable unionized voting blocs.

Maybe it's not optimal. Maybe the market left to its own devices will under-provide. As Milton Friedman and so many others have argued with respect to education, this might be an argument for government subsidy. It is not an argument for government provision.

**Police protection**. In his 2015 book *Private Governance*, Trinity College economist Edward Stringham explores the ways that (wait for it) *private governance* has evolved in markets for financial securities on stock exchanges and property protection in cities like San Francisco. As he puts it, "Judges, police, and regulators are a deus ex machina" in a lot of social scientific theorizing. And what is a *deus ex machina*? It is "a person or thing (as in fiction or drama) that appears or is introduced suddenly and unexpectedly and provides a contrived solution to an apparently insoluble difficulty."[41] If you grew up watching *Inspector Gadget* cartoons as I did, you might think of it in terms of a simple incantation: "go go gadget *government!*" Our gods from the machine, however, have their own incentives and goals that are far too often not well-aligned with the common good.

We rely, however, on private provision of rules and enforcement all the time. Disney, for example, has its own police force at Disney World. Malls and banks have security guards. Bars have bouncers. Amazon, eBay, and other online retailers have terms of service and technologies that allow them to process thousands of transactions every *second*. We don't have to imagine private rule provision and police protection. We can see it all around us.

Once again, the free market left to its own devices might not provide the "optimal" amount. If this is the case, though, then policing vouchers would be preferable to government provision.

**Welfare**. We also see private welfare all around us—indeed, our charitable impulses are so strong that there is a small cottage industry of commentary on the "second disaster" in which a flood of borderline-useless emergency relief supplies lands in a disaster-stricken area and gets in the way of the people who are doing the most effective work. After the 2010 Haiti earthquake, NYU's Development Research Institute published a very useful post entitled "Nobody wants your old shoes: How not to help in Haiti."[42]

There are a couple of replies to this. First, there's a strong argument to be made that a weaker state would mean fewer people needing welfare in the first place. In a 2013 paper in the *Journal of Economic Growth*, John W. Dawson and John J. Seater point out that a growing regulatory state has meant lower productivity growth and, therefore, lower standards of living ($0 version of their paper here). They attribute the productivity growth slowdown that began in the 1970s to changes in regulation, and this makes a certain degree of sense in light of the regulatory "victories" of the 1970s like the Environmental Protection Agency and the Occupational Safety and Health Administration.

Even then, there is a lot of evidence that historically, we have done a pretty good job of taking care of one another. First, there's the institution of the family. Adult children can take care of their aging parents, and they typically have. Even then, people could undoubtedly earn a much higher return on investment by putting the share of their earnings that is going into Social Security into the stock market. Second, there is the private sector. The historian David Beito's *From Mutual Aid to the Welfare State* and the economist John E. Murray's *Origins of American Health Insurance* explore how friendly societies, mutual aid societies, and other private-sector organizations provided formal and informal insurance in the years before the welfare state. Industrial sickness funds, Murray argues, handled medical issues reasonably well, and he argues specifically that the reason the US didn't get a European-style welfare state was not because of the machinations of insurance companies but because the private alternative was working.

**Roads**. We return to the classic objection: what about the roads? Again, there are arguments for government provision or financing of roads. However, it's not at all clear roads cannot, in the main at least, be provided privately. Daniel Klein and John Majewski make this point in the context of 19th-century US turnpikes and toll roads. The economist Dan Bogart has studied transportation innovation and argues, for example, in an important 2005 paper that private "turnpike trusts increased road expenditure, rather than replacing existing or forthcoming parish expenditure."

As with police and fire services, maybe the unfettered free market doesn't provide the *optimal* amount of road or rail. But again, this is not so much an argument for government provision as it might be an argument for government subsidy—and only then if we are pretty sure the interventionist cure won't be worse than the disease.

Governments have been providing fire protection, police services, roads, and other public services for pretty much our entire lives. If you have never known a world in which the government hasn't provided it, then it's understandable that you might not think it is possible for the market to do it. These examples, at least, are useful proofs of concept. The next time you wonder "who will build the roads" or "who will fight the fires" or "who will fight the bad guys" or "who will take care of the poor and indigent," remember that free people in free markets have a pretty good track record.

## 48

# Lobbying: Like Robbing a Record Store

In the 1990s, I was seasonally employed at Camelot Music, a store that sold cassettes, CDs, videos, posters, and so on. In 2007, I visited Northland Plaza in Columbus, Ohio, where the store was located, and found to my dismay that it is now one with Nineveh and Tyre. My time there taught me an early lesson on the costs of successful theft and the costs of successful rent-seeking—which in most cases are practically the same thing.

One day, I arrived at work and was told by a manager to watch a particular customer because they thought he was trying to steal something. For about *two hours*, the customer would wander through the store, pick things up, wander around with them, put them back, and so on.

Finally, he took a small stack of items to the cash register to check out. After the cashier had tallied his total, he picked up an item—Janet

---

Carden, Art. 2019. "Lobbying Is Like Robbing a Record Store." American Institute for Economic Research. February 26.

Jackson's *Design of the Decade* CD—said "I think I need to put this back," and bolted out the door with it.

I was angry and puzzled. The guy had spent two hours (at least) and stolen a single CD. He could have spent about two or three hours working at a minimum wage job and earned enough money to buy the CD. Perhaps he had designs on a larger haul but was thwarted by the store's eagle-eyed employees. Perhaps he had confederates who successfully made off with a large haul while he had everyone distracted. Regardless, the whole episode made the world a little bit poorer.

It's not because Camelot Music shareholders lost the CD or because Camelot employees lost benefits because of theft. I recall a meeting during which we were told that shrinkage—the industry term for theft—had gotten *really* bad, that employees needed to be more watchful, and that the losses were hitting us in the form of raises and merchandise discounts and other things we weren't getting. No, the shrinkage per se is a pure transfer from the robbed to the robbers.

The social loss came from the time and energy the thief spent trying to steal and the time and energy we spent trying to stop him. The cost of the pinched Janet Jackson CD was what the thief *could have produced* with the time and energy he spent stealing the CD.

Suppose he had worked at the Donato's Pizza at the end of the block, where I occasionally went for lunch. Then he could have taken the money he earned making pizza and bought the CD. The social cost of the theft in that case was the pizza he didn't make because he was busy stealing. And even if he couldn't have gotten a job at Donato's, he could've shoveled snow or scraped windshields or done any of a number of odd jobs until he earned enough to pay for the CD.

The resources consumed in trying to prevent theft are socially costly. These include the jewel cases in which CDs and tapes were displayed for theft prevention. What else could we store employees have done had we not been watching carefully to prevent even-greater theft?

## Lobbying: Like Robbing a Record Store

Perhaps we could have made more sales. Some customer likely left the store less than fully satisfied because she didn't get the service she would have gotten had we not been watching the guy who was trying to rip us off. These, too, are among the costs of theft.

In this sense, your home security system and the cop walking the beat are social losses: they're good for you because they mean your stuff is less likely to be stolen, but you would be better off if people didn't steal and we could use these resources and labor to produce something else.

The story has an application to the economics of politics. What are the incentives, and what do they mean for general prosperity? Ask, as many economists have: do people have incentives to *trade* or incentives to *raid*? When people have incentives to trade, they have incentives to actually create wealth. When people have incentives to raid, on the other hand, they have incentives to destroy it.

Think about politicians, lobbyists, and the firms that employ them. Firms want income-increasing special privileges. These include subsidies, rules like licensing restrictions, and other barriers to entry that allow them to raise profits by raising prices and cutting output, or tariffs that protect them from foreign competition and allow them to raise profits by selling at higher prices.

The prizes they are getting—the increased profits from subsidies, restrictions, or tariffs—are like the Janet Jackson CD that was stolen from Camelot Music over 20 years ago.

Importantly, the resources firms invest in trying to get those special privileges—things like high-priced lobbyists—are like the time and energy the thief devoted to stealing the Janet Jackson CD. The firms are consuming resources, and in a way that rewards them. They are better off, the politicians who are in a sense "selling" special privileges are better off, and the lobbyists are better off.

Not all lobbying is bad, of course, and a lot of lobbying happens as part of defensive efforts to shield people from depredation just like a lot of my job at Camelot Music was theft prevention. Think of the many millions expended by the business community in the last year to beg the government not to disrupt supply chains with new tariffs.

However, whether it is offensive or defensive lobbying, they're not actually producing any new goods or services while trying to get the prize. Society is worse off to the tune of what these firms would have produced had they actually devoted those resources to creating wealth rather than simply redistributing it.

## 49

# Think Harder About Smoke on the Water and Fire in the Sky: Externalities

You yawn, stretch, and walk to the coffee shop, where you order an espresso and settle in to read some Libertarianism.org articles your friend recommended. After your first sip, you wonder at the marvel of your cup of coffee: having read something like Leonard Read's classic "I, Pencil" or having seen the short films about it, you know that no single mind contains all the knowledge embodied in a simple cup of coffee. It all comes together through decentralized exchange that lets a coffee grower in South America cooperate with a truck driver in New England he doesn't know and will never meet.

*Wait a second,* you think. *I've driven behind large trucks before. They burn diesel fuel and stink up the air with formaldehyde and sulfur dioxide and stuff like 3-methyl-2-cyclopentene-2-ol-one. I don't even know what 3-methyl-2-cyclopentene-2-ol-one is. Then there are carbon emissions, which affect*

---

Carden, Art. 2019. "What are Externalities, In the Economic Sense of the Word? In What Ways Can They Be Addressed? The Cato Institute. July 18.

*people on the other side of the world who might not even drink or grow coffee. Is there something missing from the "I, Pencil" story?*

There is, sort of. You've just described *externalities,* or costs and benefits of your actions that spill over onto people with whom you're not trading. Let's do the "I, Pencil" thing with your cup of coffee, but let's highlight the externalities.

You're drinking your coffee out of a paper cup and thinking about everything that led to it when your concentration is shattered by the coffee grinder and the espresso machine behind the counter. You look down at your cup again and think *that's one spillover. I'm sure a lot of people in this place were disturbed by the noise when the barista was making my espresso.*

And so you think further. The cups and coffee beans were shipped on an exhaust-belching truck, and maybe they were shipped from the other side of the world on an exhaust-belching container ship. Other people breathe that stuff, so there's another spillover. The cups were made in a factory. What got dumped into streams and lakes and oceans that are now not-so-safe for swimming or fishing? You think about noise again. Trees have to be harvested to make paper cups. Then you stop and think *but firms grow trees like they grow corn. If there's an uncompensated spillover, it's that timber companies are cleaning the air for us by planting so many trees—assuming that they aren't displacing other, more complex ecosystems...*Harvesting timber, though, is noisy and messy. Chainsaws are loud, and logging trucks burn fuel just like delivery trucks and container ships. There are even more negative spillovers.

You're distracted again by a wonderful smell. Someone has just ordered a croissant. You love the aroma, and it reminds you of how much you enjoy walking by bakeries and restaurants and coffee shops and how in a city like Memphis, when the wind is right, the whole city seems to smell like barbecue. A bakery or a barbecue joint can't charge passersby for enjoying wonderful smells. Externalities, therefore, aren't only negative: there are positive externalities, too.

# Think Harder About Smoke on the Water and Fire in the Sky: Externalities

*I see the problem,* you think. *When I buy a cup of coffee, I get coffee and a lot of people get paid. There are a lot of others, though, who have nothing to do with the coffee but who incur uncompensated costs in the form of diesel exhaust and others who enjoy benefits they don't have to pay for because coffee and croissants smell delicious and because the trees that are planted to make the cups and the coffee that is planted to make the coffee convert carbon dioxide into oxygen.*

You've hit on a pretty knotty social problem. In his book *The Undercover Economist,* Tim Harford describes a competitive market as a "world of truth" in which our attention to our own interests leads us to produce the right things the right way for the right people and in the right proportions. Externalities mean that we might produce too much of a thing that generates negative externalities because we don't bear all the costs and not enough of another thing that generates positive externalities because we don't capture the benefits. When we produce coffee that creates costs in excess of its benefits, we're wasting resources.

What can we do about it?

The easy answer says "find and ban the source of a negative externality" or "find and require the source of a positive externality." We see this in, for example, mandatory pollution control equipment on cars and trucks to control negative spillovers and mandatory schooling or vaccination to create positive spillovers. The problem is that command-and-control assumes there's One Right Way to control pollution when, in fact, it's hardly clear that regulators will know the least-costly way to address the externality. Again, we're wasting resources when we produce coffee that creates costs in excess of its benefits. Our experience with government regulation and systems like socialism suggests there's a good chance that command-and-control will make the inefficiencies worse, not better.

A better answer appears in most introductory economics textbooks. There's an external cost in the form of pollution and a contribution to climate change emanating from those next gallons of diesel fuel

255

that Shell and Chevron are considering producing. According to A.C. Pigou, a tax equal to that external cost will force Shell and Chevron to take those costs into consideration where they wouldn't have before. With a tax that modifies the price just a little bit, the invisible hand leads us to the right outcome.

While it's better than command-and-control, it's still incomplete. As Ronald Coase pointed out in his 1960 article "The Problem of Social Cost," externalities come from incompletely-defined property rights. What's more, it's not clear who causes the problem. After all, if someone fells trees that will eventually become cups at your local coffee shop and there is no one around to be disturbed by the noise, he has definitely made a sound—but he has created no externality. Just as it takes two people to tango, it takes two people for there to be an externality. If there's no problem until you add the second person, who's to say it's the lumberjack causing the problem, and not the person hearing the lumberjack's noise?

One problem concerns deciding who has rights to what and then letting the market go to work. In their textbook *The Economic Way of Thinking*, Paul Heyne, Peter Boettke, and David Prychitko discuss how externalities can be addressed via *negotiation*, *adjudication*, and *legislation*. *Negotiation* happens when property rights are clearly-specified and well-enforced. Think back to the logger and imagine a retiree has a cabin near where he is working. Once we know who owns the noise rights, people can bargain to a solution. If the logger has the right to use the chainsaw, then the retiree can pay him to stop. If the retiree has the right to peace and quiet, then the logger can buy a noise easement from the retiree.

Coase develops an interesting implication: the initial assignment of rights doesn't matter for the allocation of resources if transaction costs (the costs of negotiating, executing, and enforcing exchanges) are low enough. Suppose the retiree values peace and quiet at $1,000. The logger values the right to use the chainsaw at $10,000. If the logger has the right, then he runs his chainsaw. If the retiree has the right, then the logger can buy a noise easement for anything between $1,000 and $10,000. She's better off because you receive a payment that she values more highly than the peace and quiet. The logger is better off because he pays less than the $10,000 at which he values the noise rights. Negotiation gets the rights into the right hands.

It's not always clear who has what rights. Enter *adjudication*, which is how people (likely aided by courts and lawyers) learn who has which rights. A lot of people think that the idea of first-user appropriation is a reasonable way of deciding who has which rights. Think back to when you were little and had a dispute over a toy: "who had it first?" was often the decisive question. Thinking again about the logger and the retiree, it seems reasonable to ask who was there first. If the retiree was there first, then the logger has to pay for the noise rights. If the logger was there first, the retiree doesn't have a claim. Again, if transaction costs are low enough, the rights will end up in the right hands no matter where they start.

Sometimes, a conflict is difficult to resolve through adjudication. *Legislation* might be called for. In this case, the government simply decides who has the right. Sometimes, governments simply reallocate rights by legislation (taking land via eminent domain, for example). If these reallocations are credible, they need not affect economic efficiency though they will affect the distribution of wealth and might offend our sense of justice.

Externalities emerge because of poorly-defined rights and high transaction costs. One problem with Pigou's solution, as John V.C. Nye (2008) points out, is that the measured *size* of the spillover for purposes of informing a corrective tax (or subsidy) is irrelevant to the efficiency of the outcome if the kind of Coasian bargains discussed above are happening. The measured size of the noise externality in the logging example doesn't tell us whether or not we are near to or far from the optimal amount of logging. With respect to auto exhaust, for example, he points out that we need to account for existing taxes, regulations, and possible monopoly power—Gulf Oil, for example, owns a lease that allows it the exclusive right to sell gas along the Massachusetts Turnpike.[43] Presumably, one of the costs of monopoly power is that monopolists under-produce goods—but if gasoline produces negative externalities, then a competitive market will produce too much. If Gulf's market power allows it to raise prices and lower output—my few gas purchases on the Massachusetts Turnpike have been pricey, and there are certainly fewer opportunities to buy gas than along (say) I-20 between Birmingham and Atlanta—then their market power at least partially mitigates the spillover costs from burning gas. As Nye puts it (p. 32):

> Even in a world of positive transactions costs, some Coasian transfers may take place that partly mitigate the harm of the externality. Unless the Pigovian tax collector can fully account for all those transfers, any estimate of an appropriate tax based solely on the size of the externality will clearly overstate the optimally efficient tax level.

People come up with all sorts of "Coasian transfers" that obviate the "obvious" need for government intervention. Advertising supports radio and television broadcasts. The sandwich shop Jimmy John's advertises "free smells." They are willing to provide the pleasant smell of baking bread in order to increase brand awareness and attract customers. Beekeeping was alleged to be in suboptimal supply because bees pollinate fruit trees, but Steven N.S. Cheung's empirical investigation showed how beekeepers and orchard-owners contract to internalize spillover benefits.

People also form *proprietary communities* that establish rules governing externality-generating activities. Homeowners' Associations might have rules about whether or not people can paint their houses garish colors. Colleges and universities might require students to be vaccinated. Disney World has rules. And so on.

Markets do a better job with externalities than we might at first believe. Coase, in 1974, wrote an article on "The Lighthouse in Economics" that explained how lighthouse services were provided privately, and this insight was extended (and objections to Coase's thesis were addressed) by Rosolino Candela and Vincent Geloso in a 2018 study of the light*ship*, which disappeared not because of insurmountable externalities but because government squashed it.

If we're going to address externalities, we need to account for *all* the externalities, positive and negative. One person's foul odor might be another's pleasant seasonal scent (the faint smell of smoke in the Fall, for example). The same action might produce offsetting externalities. Mowing your grass is a perfect example. Power mowers are noisy, and they pollute. However, mowing your yard makes it less of a breeding ground for pests and less of a fire hazard.

Finally, we have to make sure the cure we're proposing isn't worse than the disease. I'm reminded of an old episode of *The Simpsons* in which invasive Bolivian tree lizards ended up in Springfield. Principal Skinner recanted his criticism of the lizards and called them "a godsend" because they ate pigeons. Lisa asked if this wasn't short-sighted. Principal Skinner suggested that they could "unleash wave after wave of Chinese needle snakes" in the event that the lizard population became unmanageable. Lisa replied: "but…aren't the snakes even worse?" Principal Skinner replies that they've "lined up a fabulous type of gorilla that thrives on snake meat." When Lisa protests that they would then be "stuck with gorillas," Principal Skinner points to "the beautiful part: when winter time rolls around, the gorillas simply freeze to death"—leaving the town buried under rotting gorilla carcasses.

Externalities are everywhere. Part of living in a civilized society is developing the ability to live with a thousand little annoyances because frankly, you're probably producing a thousand little annoyances for everyone else and we wouldn't get anything done if we tried to resolve to a standard of abstract justice every little slight real or imagined. Some spillovers are big enough and important enough that they're worth paying more attention to and perhaps even addressing with public policy. Just because an externality *exists* doesn't mean the market has "failed" enough for command-and-control regulation or even corrective taxation to be appropriate. Markets—and the institutions of civil society—have proven themselves pretty robust aids to voluntary cooperation and voluntary solutions.

## 50

# Coda: Why Economics is Crucial for Ethical Reflection

I assume we all want to use the lives we've been given to make the world a better place. This isn't as straightforward as it seems at first. It is insufficient merely to think globally, and depressingly many kinds of acting locally are positively destructive. I have been asked to consider a handful of questions: I'm supposed to discuss the most pressing issue in the world, whether it is getting better or worse, and what we can do about it. I have also been asked what we can do to reduce infant mortality in Memphis. Finally, I've been asked what "thinking globally and acting locally" means to me. I will discuss each in turn.

Poverty is the most important issue in the world because it is the ultimate arbiter of who lives and who dies. We have made a lot of progress in the last two decades, particularly with the continued integration of India and China into the global economy and increases in economic freedom in both. We have made a lot of progress, but there are still a

---

This chapter is based on remarks I prepared for a panel on "What's Wrong With the World?" at Rhodes College on September 29, 2009. It appears online here. https://mises.org/library/why-economics-crucial-ethics

lot of problems. The most important problem, I think, are unreflective activism and uninformed dissent, which stand in the way of our development as ethical people.

Come again? Did I, an economist, say "ethical?" Yes, I, an economist, said "ethical." I tell my students that economics *as such* cannot tell you which values to have, but I would argue that endeavoring to understand what careful economic reasoning can say about the world is an important part of being an ethical person because the unintended consequences of policies that fly in the face of basic economic reasoning have been tragic. The cruel irony is that poverty can be institutionalized by policies supported by allegedly well-meaning activists who don't understand the ramifications of the policies they advocate.

I encourage you, therefore, to take steps toward developing a good ethos. Avoid the presumption that other people need you to act as their moral surrogate. In one of the most famous passages in Adam Smith's *Theory of Moral Sentiments*, Smith speaks of "the man of system." It is worth quoting him at length:

> "The man of system, on the contrary, is apt to be very wise in his own conceit; and is often so enamoured with the supposed beauty of his own ideal plan of government, that he cannot suffer the smallest deviation from any part of it. He goes on to establish it completely and in all its parts, without any regard either to the great interests, or to the strong prejudices which may oppose it. He seems to imagine that he can arrange the different members of a great society with as much ease as the hand arranges the different pieces upon a chess-board. He does not consider that the pieces upon the chess-board have no other principle of motion besides that which the hand impresses upon them; but that, in the great chess-board of human society, every single piece has a principle of motion of its own,

## Coda: Why Economics is Crucial for Ethical Reflection

altogether different from that which the legislature might chuse to impress upon it. If those two principles coincide and act in the same direction, the game of human society will go on easily and harmoniously, and is very likely to be happy and successful. If they are opposite or different, the game will go on miserably, and the society must be at all times in the highest degree of disorder." Paragraph VI.II.42

In modern parlance, don't be "that guy." When you identify a source of social tension, realize that the source of the tension might not be the ignorance, idiocy, or venality of the people you want to control but your desire to control them. Don't think that you have all of the answers, and avoid being motivated by self-congratulation. Sincere good wishes will not prevent a policy's consequences (both desirable and undesirable). We're all sincere, presumably, but you can't get justice and prosperity merely by wishing for it. Again, this is a deadly serious issue. Part of becoming a responsible adult—a status that a lot of people fail to achieve, sadly—is dropping the expectation that you will be let off the hook for the consequences of your actions because you meant well or because you didn't intend to do harm. Economists are criticized sometimes because we don't consider ethical issues in economic analysis *per se*, but a similar charge is perhaps more accurately cast at our critics. Here is Steven Horwitz (2009) on the intersection between ethics and economics:

> It might be more accurate to say that ethicists ignore economics than that economists ignore ethics. To the extent that good economics shows what we can and cannot do with social policy, it is engaged with ethics. After all, if the point of saying we ought to do X is that we think it will achieve some set of morally desirable goals, then knowing whether or not doing X

will actually achieve those goals is, or at least should be, a key part of moral inquiry.

Sheldon Richman from the Foundation for Economic Education has described a similar tendency—to focus on moral goals without considering whether the policies we advocate will achieve those goals—as the intellectual equivalent of drunk driving. No drunk driver gets behind the wheel of a car *intending* to cause damage or death. Similarly, no one advocates an increase in the minimum wage *intending* to cut the bottom off the economic ladder and make it *harder* to escape poverty. When a drunk driver causes a highway death, whether he or she *intended* to kill someone is irrelevant to the fact that it happened. When raising the minimum wage shuts poor people out of the labor market, whether advocates of the minimum wage *intend* for that to happen is also irrelevant.

Economics reasoning helps us expose absurdities in seemingly noble moral pronouncements. Here are two examples. The Queen of England excoriated economists for being unable to see the Great Recession coming. William Easterly pointed out that we actually did better than predicting the crisis. We predicted that we wouldn't be able to predict it. Hindsight is 20/20 and saying "yes, asset prices were wrong" is not an indictment of economics or of financial markets.

We can theorize about the general conditions under which recessions occur, but we can't systematically predict the specifics of crises, panics, and other disasters because anyone who can has an incentive to act on and profit from his or her superior insight. If you are making money hand over fist exploiting inefficiencies in the market, then I will believe you and listen to your criticisms of efficient markets. Until then, I've seen nothing to suggest that markets are systematically inefficient in a knowable, predictable way.

Here is a second example. You have perhaps heard a commentator say that the problem with business is that it only thinks about the short run. Executives only care about the next quarter's earnings report. This is wrong. Companies and corporations are bound to have long-run time horizons because the price of a stock represents the discounted present value of earnings accruing to the firm's assets. Making decisions that increase short-run profitability at the expense of long-run profitability will lower the value of the firm's assets and, therefore, reduce the price of the firm's stock. If you think that you have correctly identified such a situation, then the proper response is not a condemnation of the firm and its unethical executives but a leveraged buyout. If markets are allowed to function, the notion of an undue focus on the short run is not a valid criticism of businesses.

It is, however, a valid criticism of political action because profit-maximizing firms and political actors face different incentives. I am a residual claimant to the profits generated by the firms in which I hold stock. I am not a residual claimant to anything held by the government. I have the incentive to see that the firms in which I am a stockholder manage my money wisely. I have less-powerful incentives to see that the government does not waste resources. Further, the principal-agent problem inherent in any hierarchy is less pronounced in the private sector than it is in the government. Executives and mid-level managers who mis-manage my money can be fired and replaced without too much difficulty. It is much more difficult to get rid of politicians and bureaucrats who have vague objectives and who cannot engage in rational economic calculation because they are not disciplined by prices, profits, and losses.

Prices, profits, and losses send clear signals. To adopt a vivid but not-entirely-correct metaphor, losses are the blood in the water of shark-infested financial markets: stop bleeding, or you will be devoured.

So what of "thinking globally" and "acting locally"? The best thing you can do "locally" is to try as hard as you can to understand the world around you. I would argue that this requires intensive and careful study of economics (which is the logic of choice) and probability (which is the language of science). In everything, remember to do justice, love mercy, and *walk humbly with your God*. The operative word here is not justice or mercy, but "humbly." A lot of people have failed to walk humbly. In the process, they have caused untold suffering.

My outlook is not based on naive assumptions about human goodness or about Pollyanna-ish ideas about markets producing utopia, but on my conviction that I haven't the wisdom to claim the right to substitute by force my judgment for someone else's. Those who have claimed this prerogative historically have been the source of great pain and suffering. The world today is richer than it has ever been. Nonetheless, governments that were "very wise in (their) own conceit" killed about a quarter of a billion people in the twentieth century. History gives lots of space to the great thinkers and innovators of the last couple of centuries, and I don't want to take away from their achievements. But how many great thinkers and innovators perished in the gulags? How many died in slave ships? How many are buried in mass graves somewhere? We will never know.

Let's get specific and consider infant mortality. Make sure you have your facts straight, and make sure you are comparing apples to apples. International infant mortality comparisons can be adulterated by different definitions of infant mortality across countries. What is counted as a live birth in the US might be counted as a stillbirth in (say) the United Kingdom. Thus, our ability to draw meaningful inferences from international infant mortality data is hindered. Furthermore, you can construct an example in which everyone is strictly better off but in which measured infant mortality increases while measured life expectancy falls. If maternal health improves slightly, babies who would have been miscarried will be carried to term, where they might die early. This will increase infant mortality and reduce life expectancy at birth. Furthermore, they are likely to be more susceptible to disease, which means that disease prevalence will likely increase. If the debate over health care has taught me anything, it is that we do not know enough about demography to be able to make the kinds of statements so many people are making so cavalierly in the national media.

So what do we do about it if we wish to "think globally" and "act locally?" Fortunately, there is a lot of low-hanging fruit. We spend a lot of time in economics classes talking about the unintended negative consequences of different policies. Policies that should be fought and repealed include pretty much any interference with the market process: minimum wages, price controls, taxes, and subsidies should all be repealed. Why? One reason is that we can show how they waste resources by encouraging activities for when the costs exceed the benefits and discouraging activities for which the benefits exceed the costs. Further, to the degree that they put piles of money on the table that are just up for grabs, they encourage wasteful expenditures trying to get those piles of money not by creating value but by securing political advantage. At this point it no doubt seems like economists are the wet blankets of the world, but one of the most important implications of careful economic reasoning is that often, your schemes and programs will not just be ineffective, they will be positively destructive.

# REFERENCES AND FURTHER READING

Austin, Sophie, and Louis Jacobson. 2019. "Does the U.S. Women's Soccer Team Bring in More Revenue but Get Paid Less Than the Men?" Politifact. July 11.

Backman, Rachel. 2019. "U.S. Women's Soccer Games Outearned Men's Games." Wall Street Journal. June 17.

Bailey, Ronald. 2015. The End of Doom: Environmental Renewal in the Twenty-first Century. London: Macmillan.

Baptist, Edward E. 2016. The Half Has Never Been Told: Slavery and the Making of American Capitalism. London: Hachette UK.

Barry, Norman. 1982. "The Tradition of Spontaneous Order." Literature of Liberty, V(2): 1-58.

Barzel, Yoram. 1974. "A Theory of Rationing by Waiting." The Journal of Law and Economics 17.1: 73-95.

Barzel, Yoram. 2002. A Theory of the State: Economic Rights, Legal Rights, and the Scope of the State. Cambridge, England: Cambridge University Press.

Bastiat, Frederic. 2015. "That Which Is Seen and that Which Is Not Seen." Foundation for Economic Education. May 29.

Baumol, William. 2002. The Free-Market Innovation Machine. Princeton: Princeton University Press.

Beckert, Sven. 2015. Empire of Cotton: A Global History. New York: Vintage.

Beito, David T. 2000. From Mutual Aid to the Welfare State: Fraternal Societies and Social Services, 1890-1967. Univ of North Carolina Press.

Bennett, Stephanie. 2019. Barbers Protest Bill That Would End License and Education Required to Cut Hair. ABC7. March 6.

Bloom, Allen. 2008. Closing of the American Mind. New York City: Simon and Schuster.

Bogart, Dan. 2005. "Did Turnpike Trusts Increase Transportation Investment in Eighteenth-Century England?." Journal of Economic History: 439-468.

Boudreaux, Donald. 2016. The Prosperity Pool. The Library of Economics and Liberty. Apr 4.

Boudreaux, Donald J. 2019. "The State Is Not a Transcendental Being." American Institute for Economic Research. March 18.

Boudreaux, Donald J. and Veronique De Rugy. 2019. "James M. Buchanan: A Centenary Appreciation." American Institute for Economic Research. September 26.

Brennan, Jason, and Phillip Magness. 2019. Cracks in the Ivory Tower: The Moral Mess of Higher Education. Oxford: Oxford University Press.

Briggs, Zack. 2019. Bill Would Abolish Arkansas Barber Board, No License or Education Required to Cut Hair. ABC7. March 5.

Britschigi, Christian. 2018. "San Francisco Man Has Spent 4 Years and $1 Million Trying to Get Approval to Turn His Own Laundromat Into an Apartment Building." Reason. February 21.

Buchanan, James M. 1982. "Order defined in the process of its emergence." Literature of liberty 5.5: 7-58.

Buchanan, James M. 1994. Ethics and Economic Progress. Norman: University of Oklahoma Press.

Buchanan, James, David Gordon, and Israel Kirzner. 1982. "Readers' Forum, Comments on 'The Tradition of Spontaneous Order' by Norman Barry." The Library of Economics and Liberty.

Bureau of Labor Statistics. 2020. "Barbers, Hairstylists, and Cosmetologists." Occupational Outlook Handbook. October 16.

Candela, Rosolino and Vincent Geloso. 2018. The Lightship in Economics. Public Choice 176(3):479-506.

Caplan, Bryan. 2007. The Myth of the Rational Voter: Why Democracies Choose Bad Policies. Princeton, NJ: Princeton University Press.

Caplan, Bryan. 2010. Foreword to Eugen Richter, Pictures of the Socialistic Future. Auburn, AL: Ludwig von Mises Institute.

Caplan, Bryan. 2011. Selfish Reasons to Have More Kids: Why being a great parent is less work and more fun than you think. New York City: Basic Books.

Caplan, Bryan. 2012. "The Myth of the Rational Voter and Political Theory." Collective Wisdom: Principles and Mechanisms: 319-37.

Caplan, Brian. 2018. "Socialists Without a Plan." Econ Log. October 31.

Caplan, Bryan. 2018. The Case Against Education: Why the education system is a waste of time and money. Princeton, NJ: Princeton University Press.

Caplan, Bryan. 2019. "A One-Page Hop from Bleeding Heart to Mailed Fist." The Library of Economics and Liberty. Feb 4.

Caplan, Bryan and Zach Weinersmith. 2019. Open Borders: The Science and Ethics of Immigration. New York: First Second.

Caton, James L. 2019. "Keynes Didn't Invent Aggregate Analysis." American Institute for Economic Research. March 27.

Cheung, Steven N.S. 1973. The Fable of the Bees: An Economic Investigation. Journal of Law and Economics 16:11-33.

Christian, Jon. 2018. "People Are Refusing to Use Self-Checkout Because It'll 'Kill Jobs'." Futurism. December 9.

Clemens, Jeffrey, Lisa B. Kahn, and Jonathan Meer. 2018. The Minimum Wage, Fringe Benefits, and Worker Welfare. No. w24635. National Bureau of Economic Research.

Coase, Ronald H. 1960. "The Problem of Social Cost." Classic Papers in Natural Resource Economics. London: Palgrave Macmillan. 87-137.

Cowen, Tyler. 2008. Create Your Own Economy: The Path to Prosperity in a Disordered World. London, UK. Penguin.

Cowen, Tyler. 2019. Big Business: A Love Letter to an American Anti-Hero. New York City: St. Martin's Press.

Currie-Knight, Kevin. 2019. Education in the Marketplace: An Intellectual History of Pro-Market Libertarian Visions for Education in Twentieth Century America. New York: Springer.

Dawson, John W., and John J. Seater. 2013. "Federal Regulation and Aggregate Economic Growth." Journal of Economic Growth 18.2: 137-177.

Desrochers, Pierre, and Joanna Szurmak. 2018. Population Bombed!: Exploding the Link Between Overpopulation and Climate Change. London: Global Warming Policy Foundation.

Ehrlich, Paul. 1968. The Population Bomb. New York: Ballantine Book Publication.

Engerman, Stanley L. 2017. "Review of The Business of Slavery and the Rise of American Capitalism, 1815-1860 by Calvin Schermerhorn and The Half Has Never Been Told: Slavery and the Making of American Capitalism by Edward E. Baptist." Journal of Economic Literature 55.2: 637-43.

Epstein, Gene. 2020. "Anatomy of the Great Suppression." American Institute for Economic Research. April 13.

Friedman, David. 1997. Hidden Order. New York: Harper Business.

Gill, Anthony. 2019. "Dear Billionaires, the US Treasury Awaits Your Voluntary Contribution." American Institute for Economic Research. July 1.

Glickman, Lawrence B. 2019. Free Enterprise: An American History. New Haven, Connecticut: Yale University Press.

Glynn, John. 2019. "Yes, There Is A Soccer Pay Gap: The Women Make More Than The Men." The Federalist. July 8.

Goldberg, Jonah. 2018. Suicide of the West: How the rebirth of tribalism, populism, nationalism, and identity politics is destroying American democracy. New York: Crown Forum.

Hansen, Bradley A. 2014. "The Back of Ed Baptist's Envelope." Bradley A. Hansen's Blog. October 30.

Hartsman, Avery. 2020. "San Francisco Startups Have Suspended Sales of At-Home Coronavirus Test Kits After the FDA Issued a Warning." Business Insider. March 24.

Hayek, F. A. 2015. "The Essence of the Road to Serfdom (in Cartoons!)." Foundation for Economic Freedom. August 7.

Hayek, Friedrich A. 1945. The Use of Knowledge in Society. American Economic Review 35(4):519-530.

Hayek, Friedrich August. 2013. The Fatal Conceit: The Errors of Socialism. Abingdon, UK: Routledge.

Heilbroner, Robert L. 2008. Socialism. Concise Encyclopedia of Economics.

Henderson, David. 2000. "The Case for Sweatshops." Hoover Institute. February 7.

Henderson, David. 2019. "Letter to the Presidential Candidates: It's Time to Tax Others More." The Library of Economics and Liberty. June 25.

Henderson, David. 2020. "Liberation From Lockdown Now." American Institute for Economic Research. April 13.

Henderson, M. Todd, and Salen Churi. 2019. The Trust Revolution. Cambridge, England: Cambridge University Press.

Heyne, Paul T., Peter J. Boettke, and David L. 1994. Prychitko.1994. The Economic Way of Thinking. Prentice Hall.

Heyne, Paul. 2008. Are Economists Basically Immoral? Indianapolis: Liberty Fund.

Higgs, Robert. 1987. Crisis and leviathan. New York: Oxford University Press.

Hilt, Eric. 2017. "Economic History, Historical Analysis, and the 'New History of Capitalism'." The Journal of Economic History. 77.2: 511-536.

# References and Further Reading

Holcombe, Randall. 2007. Entrepreneurship and Economic Progress. Abingdon, UK: Routledge.

Holcombe, Randall G. 2018. Political Capitalism: How political influence is made and maintained. Cambridge, England: Cambridge University Press.

Holmes, Arthur Frank. 1987. The Idea of a Christian College. Grand Rapids, Michigan: Wm. B. Eerdmans Publishing.

Horwitz, Steven. 2009. "Ought Implies Can." Foundation for Economic Freedom. April 24.

Huemer, Michael. 2013. The Problem of Political Authority. London: Palgrave MacMillan.

Hutt, William Harold. 1977. The Theory of Idle Resources. Auburn, Alabama: Ludwig von Mises Institute.

IRS. 2018. "IRS Issues Standard Mileage Rates for 2019." IRS. December 14.

Jacobson, Brigitte. 2019. "Use self-checkout? You are part of the problem." The Baltimore. June 3.

Johnson, Walter. 2013. River of Dark Dreams. Cambridge, MA: Harvard University Press.

Johnston, Max. 2019. "Michigan Cherry Farmers Celebrate New Turkish Tariffs." Interlochen Public Radio. September 23.

Juma, Calestous. 2016. Innovation and It's Enemies: Why people resist new technologies. Oxford, England: Oxford University Press.

Keynes, John Maynard. The General Theory of Employment, Interest, and Money. New York: Springer, 2018.

Klein, Daniel B. 2005. "The People's Romance: Why People Love Government (as much as they do)." The Independent Review 10.1: 5-37.

Klein, Daniel B., and John Majewski. 2008. "Turnpikes and Toll Roads in Nineteenth-Century America." EH. Net Encyclopedia.

Landsburg, Steven. 2004. "What I Like About Scrooge." Slate. December 9.

Landsburg, Steven E. 2007. The Armchair Economist: Economics & Everyday Life. New York City: Simon and Schuster.

Landsburg, Steven. 2013. Price Theory and Applications. Boston, Massachusets. Cengage Learning.

Landsburg, Steve. 2016. "Trumponomics." The Big Questions. June 28.

Lewis, C.S. 1991. The Four Loves. Boston: Houghton Mifflin Harcourt.

Lewis, C.S. 2001. The Abolition of Man. Grand Rapids: Zondervan.

Lukianoff, Greg, and Jonathan Haidt. 2015. "The Coddling of the American Mind." The Atlantic 316.2: 42-52.

Lukianoff, G., Haidt, J. 2018. The Coddling of the American Mind: How Good Intentions and Bad Ideas Are Setting Up a Generation for Failure. United Kingdom: Penguin Publishing Group.

Magness, Phillip. 2017. "Buchanan's Position on Vouchers and Segregation: The Documents MacLean Missed." Phillip W. Magness. Oct 23.

Margo, Robert A. 2018. "The Integration of Economic History into Economics." Cliometrica 12.3: 377-406.

Marx, Karl. 1846. "Letter from Marx to Pavel Vasilyevich Annenkov." Marx Engels Collected Works 38. December 28.

Marx, Karl and Friedrich Engels. 1848. Manifesto of the Communist Party. Moscow: Progress Publishers.

McCarraher, Eugene. 2019. The Enchantments of Mammon: How Capitalism Became the Religion of Modernity. Cambridge, Massachusetts: Harvard University Press.

McChesney, Fred S. 1986. "Government Prohibitions on Volunteer Fire Fighting in Nineteenth-Century America: A Property Rights Perspective." The Journal of Legal Studies 15.1: 69-92.

McChesney, Fred S. 2002. "Smoke and Errors." The Library of Economics and Liberty. June 24.

McCloskey, Deirdre N. 2006. The Bourgeois Virtues: Ethics for an Age of Commerce. Chicago: University of Chicago Press.

McCloskey, Deirdre N. 2010. Bourgeois Dignity: Why Economics Can't Explain the Modern World. Chicago: University of Chicago Press.

McCloskey, Deirdre Nansen. 2016. Bourgeois Equality: How Ideas, Not Capital or Institutions, Enriched the World. Chicago: University of Chicago Press.

McGeehan, Patrick. 2019. "After Winning a $15 Minimum Wage, Fast Food Workers Now Battle Unfair Firings." New York Times. February 12.

McMaken, Ryan. 2019. "Consumers Will Decide If Women's Sports Teams Get 'Equal Pay'." Mises Wire. July 11.

Metzger, Andy. 2016. "Gulf to Remain Mass. Pike Gas Provider Until 2025." Boston Business Journal. November 22.

Mises, Ludwig von. 1920. Economic Calculation in the Socialist Commonwealth. Auburn, AL: Ludwig von Mises Institute.

Mises, Ludwig von. 1949. Human Action. Auburn, AL: Ludwig von Mises Institute.

Mises, Ludwig von. 1951. Socialism: An Economic and Sociological Analysis. Auburn, AL: Ludwig von Mises Institute.

Mokyr, Joel. 2009. The Enlightened Economy: An Economic History of Britain, 1700-1850. New Haven: Yale University Press.

Mokyr, Joel. 2016. *A Culture of Growth: The Origins of the Modern Economy*. Princeton: Princeton University Press.

Munger, Michael. 2006. "Rent-Seek and You Will Find." *The Library of Economics and Liberty*. July 3.

Munger, Michael. 2007. "Munger on Price Gouging." American Institute for Economic Research. January 8.

Munger, Michael C. 2018. *Tomorrow 3.0: Transaction costs and the sharing economy*. Cambridge, England: Cambridge University Press.

Munger, Michael. 2018. "Will Reducing Transaction Costs Be the End of Retail?" *American Institute for Economic Research*. December 19.

Munger, Michael. 2019. "The Future of Public Goods." American Institute for Economic Research. June 6.

Murray, Harold, and James Ruthven. 1913. *A History of Chess*. Oxford: Clarendon Press.

Niemietz, Kristian. 2019. *Socialism: The Failed Idea That Never Dies*. London: London Publishing Partnership.

Nordhaus, William D. 1996. "Do real-output and real-wage measures capture reality? The history of lighting suggests not." *The economics of new goods*. University of Chicago Press. 27-70.

North, Douglass C. Prize Lecture. 2020. *NobelPrize.org*. Nobel Media AB 2020. Nov 2.

North, Douglass C. 2005. *Understanding the Process of Economic Cha*nge. Princeton: Princeton University Press.

Nye, John VC. 2008. "The Pigou Problem." George Mason University. Regulation 31: 32.

Olmstead, Alan L., and Paul W. Rhode. 2018. "Cotton, Slavery, and the New History of Capitalism." Explorations in Economic History 67: 1-17.

Otteson, James R. 2010. "Adam Smith and the Great Mind Fallacy." Social Philosophy and Policy 27(1):276-304.

Otteson, James R. 2019. Honorable Business: A Framework for Business in a Just and Humane Society. Oxford, England: Oxford University Press.

Otteson, James. 2014. The End of Socialism. Cambridge, MA: Cambridge University Press, 2014.

Paterson, Isabel. 1993. The God of the Machine. Piscataway, NJ: Transaction Publishers.

Pisani, Joseph. 2018. "Amazon to Cut Bonuses, Stock Benefits as it Raises Wages." AP News. October 3.

Rauch, Jonathan. 1993. Kindly Inquisitors: The New Attacks on Free Thought. Chicago: University of Chicago Press.

Read, Leonard. 1958. I, Pencil: My family tree as told to Leonard E. New York City: Freeman.

Richter, Eugen. 1983. Pictures of the Socialistic Future. Auburn, AL: Ludwig von Mises Institute.

Ridley, Matt. 2010. The Rational Optimist: How Prosperity Evolves. New York: Harper.

Rose, David C. 2011. The Moral Foundation of Economic Behavior. Oxford, England: Oxford University Press.

Rose, David C. 2018. Why Culture Matters Most. Oxford, England: Oxford University Press.

Rosling, Hans. 2019. Factfulness. New York: Flatiron.

Saunders, Peter. 2007. "Why capitalism is good for the soul." Policy: A Journal of Public Policy and Ideas 23.4: 3.

Schumpeter, Joseph A. 2013. Capitalism, Socialism and Democracy. Abingdon, UK: Routledge.

Scott, James C. 1998. Seeing Like a State. New Haven: The Yale ISPS series.

Scott, James C. 2010. "The Trouble with the View from Above." Cato Unbound. September 8.

Scott, James C. 2010. The Art of Not Being Governed: An Anarchist History of Upland Southeast Asia. New Haven: Yale University Press.

Scott, James C. 2017. Against the Grain: A Deep History of the Earliest States. New Haven: Yale University Press, 2017.

Shaikh, Alanna. 2010. "Nobody wants your old shoes: How not to help in Haiti." Aid Watch Blog. January 16.

Simon, Julian L. 1981. The Ultimate Resource. Princeton, NJ: Princeton University Press.

Smith, Adam. 1759. The Theory of Moral Sentiments. London: A. Millar.

Smith, Adam. 1827. An Inquiry Into the Nature and Causes of the Wealth of Nations. Edinburgh: T. Nelson and P. Brown.

Snyder, Benjamin. 2015. "There's a Huge Pay Disparity Between Male and Female Supermodels." Fortune. July 15.

Sowell, Thomas. 2002. Applied economics: Thinking Beyond Stage One. London: Hachette UK.

Stokes, Allen. 2019. "Pets on Patios: are they allowed in Alabama?" News 19. July 10.

Stringham, Edward. 2009. "Private Policing in San Francisco." Independent Institute. December 21.

Stringham, Edward. 2015. Private Governance. Oxford: Oxford University Press.

Sun-Tzu. 1963. The Art of War. London: Oxford University Press.

Tallis, Raymond. 2011. Rethinking Thinking. Wall Street Journal. November 12.

Tett, Lyn. 1996. "Education and the Marketplace." The Learning Society: Challenges and Trends: 150-161.

Thale, Christopher. 2005. "Haymarket and May Day." The Electronic Encyclopedia of Chicago.

Thornton-O'Connel, Jodi. 2017. "What Average Americans Spend on Groceries—See How You Stack Up." Go BankingRates. September 14.

Tucker, Jeffrey. 2019. The Market Loves You: Why You Should Love it Back. Great Barrington, Massachusetts: American Institute for Economic Research.

Tullock, Gordon. 1967. "The Welfare Costs of Tariffs, Monopolies, and Theft." Economic Inquiry 5.3: 224-232.

Weaver, Richard M. 2013. Ideas Have Consequences: Expanded Edition. Chicago: University of Chicago Press.

Wright, Gavin. 2020. "Slavery and Anglo-American Capitalism Revisited." The Economic History Review. 73.2: 353-383.

Wright, Robert E. 2017. The Poverty of Slavery: How Unfree Labor Pollutes the Economy. New York: Springer.

Zagoria, Adam. 2018. "Could Duke's Zion Williamson Earn $1 Billion In His Basketball Career?" Forbes. Nov 23.

# ENDNOTES

1. Carden, Art. 2019. "The Prosperity Around You Is the Fruit of the Enlightenment." American Institute for Economic Research. July 28.
2. http://www.fnal.gov/pub/science/inquiring/questions/atoms.html, last accessed December 5, 2020.
3. https://www.quora.com/How-long-will-it-be-until-we-run-out-of-combinations-of-notes-for-a-classical-music-composition, last accessed December 5, 2020.
4. https://en.wikipedia.org/wiki/History_of_chess
5. Carden, Art. 2018. The Invisible Hand Brings Me Almonds. Forbes.com Apr 16.
6. Stokes, Allen. 2019. "Pets on Patios: are they allowed in Alabama?" News 19. July 10.
7. Briggs, Zack. 2019. Bill Would Abolish Arkansas Barber Board, No License or Education Required to Cut Hair. ABC7. March 5.
8. Bennett, Stephanie. 2019. Barbers Protest Bill That Would End License and Education Required to Cut Hair. ABC7. March 6.
9. Landsburg, Steve. 2016. "Trumponomics." The Big Questions. June 28.
10. Bureau of Labor Statistics. 2020. "Barbers, Hairstylists, and Cosmetologists." Occupational Outlook Handbook. October 16.
11. IRS. 2018. "IRS Issues Standard Mileage Rates for 2019." IRS. December 14.
12. Carden, Art. 2018. "How Can You Get Other People To Work For You?" Forbes. October 25.
13. Boudreaux, Donald J. 2019. "The State Is Not a Transcendental Being." American Institute for Economic Research. March 18.

14. Thale, Christopher. 2005. "Haymarket and May Day." The Electronic Encyclopedia of Chicago.
15. Niemietz, Kristian. 2019. Socialism: The Failed Idea That Never Dies. London: London Publishing Partnership, 2019.
16. See Caton, James L. 2019. "Keynes Didn't Invent Aggregate Analysis." American Institute for Economic Research. March 27.
17. Thornton-O'Connel, Jodi. 2017. "What Average Americans Spend on Groceries — See How You Stack Up." Go BankingRates. September 14.
18. Snyder, Benjamin. 2015. "There's a Huge Pay Disparity Between Male and Female Supermodels." Fortune. July 15.
19. Ozanian, Mike. 2019. World Cup Soccer Pay Disparity Between Men and Women is Justified. Forbes.com March 7. Backman, Rachel. 2019. "U.S. Women's Soccer Games Outearned Men's Games." Wall Street Journal. June 17.
20. Glynn, John. 2019. "Yes, There Is A Soccer Pay Gap: The Women Make More Than The Men." The Federalist. July 8.
21. McMaken, Ryan. 2019. "Consumers Will Decide If Women's Sports Teams Get 'Equal Pay'." Mises Wire. July 11.
22. Johnston, Max. 2019. "Michigan Cherry Farmers Celebrate New Turkish Tariffs." Interlochen Public Radio. September 23.
23. Currie-Knight, Kevin. 2019. Education in the Marketplace: An Intellectual History of Pro-Market Libertarian Visions for Education in Twentieth Century America. New York: Springer
24. Scott, James C. 2010. "The Trouble with the View from Above." Cato Unbound. September 8.
25. McGeehan, Patrick. 2019. "After Winning a $15 Minimum Wage, Fast Food Workers Now Battle Unfair Firings." New York Times. February 12.
26. Pisani, Joseph. 2018. "Amazon to Cut Bonuses, Stock Benefits as it Raises Wages." AP News. October 3.
27. https://www.labor.ny.gov/workerprotection/laborstandards/workprot/minwage.shtm
28. Hartsman, Avery. 2020. "San Francisco Startups Have Suspended Sales of At-Home Coronavirus Test Kits After the FDA Issued a Warning." Business Insider. March 24.
29. https://www.annualreports.com/HostedData/AnnualReportArchive/c/NASDAQ_CRAY_2009.pdf
30. Britschigi, Christian. 2018. "San Francisco Man Has Spent 4 Years and $1 Million Trying to Get Approval to Turn His Own Laundromat Into an Apartment Building." Reason. February 21.

# Endnotes

**31.** https://sftu.org/rent-control/

**32.** See the Concise Encylopedia of Economics entry on rent control: http://www.econlib.org/library/Enc/RentControl.html

**33.** Marx, Karl. 1846. "Letter from Marx to Pavel Vasilyevich Annenkov." Marx Engels Collected Works 38. December 28.

**34.** Bradley A. Hansen. 2014. "The Back of Ed Baptist's Envelope." Bradley A. Hansen's Blog. October 30.

**35.** Caplan, Brian. 2018. "Socialists Without a Plan." Econ Log. October 31.

**36.** "Lenin and the First Communist Revolutions, I" Museum of Communism. Online.

**37.** Cowen, Tyler. 2019. Big Business: A Love Letter to an American Anti-Hero. New York City: St. Martin's Press.

**38.** The Onion. 2019. "Duke Anthropology Professor Devastated To Learn Promising Student Dropping Out." The Onion. April 12.

**39.** Zagoria, Adam. 2018. "Could Duke's Zion Williamson Earn $1 Billion In His Basketball Career?" Forbes. Nov 23.

**40.** Carden, Art. 2010. "Fight My Fire: Government or the Market?" Forbes. October 8.

**41.** https://www.merriam-webster.com/dictionary/deus%20ex%20machina

**42.** Shaikh, Alanna. 2010. "Nobody wants your old shoes: How not to help in Haiti." Aid Watch Blog. January 16.

**43.** Metzger, Andy. 2016. "Gulf to Remain Mass. Pike Gas Provider Until 2025." Boston Business Journal. November 22.

# INDEX

achievement, 31–32, 146
American, 19, 31, 142, 153–154, 159, 162, 199, 201, 204–206, 208–209, 217, 219, 221, 223, 246
anthropology, 235–237
Apple, 27, 74, 78–80, 119–120
Arkansans, 97, 99–100

Bailey, Ronald, 34
bankers, 206, 233
Baptist, Edward E., 206-207
Barzel, Yoram, 61, 142, 176
Bastiat, Frederic, 120, 137
Baumol, William, 28
Beito, David T., 246
Black Friday, 133–135
Bloom, Allen, 199
Boettke, Peter J., 134, 256
borders, 49, 150–152
Boston, 33, 65–66, 225
Boudreaux, Donald, 1, 48, 107
Brennan, Jason, 160
Buchanan, James M., 19, 54, 56, 88, 134-135, 168, 171, 188-189
business, 7, 35, 50, 53-54, 58, 89, 98–99, 102, 106, 111, 114, 121, 154, 176, 188–189, 217–219, 222–223, 233–234, 252, 264-265

capitalism/capitalist, 16, 31–33, 89, 91, 126, 150, 205–206, 209
Caplan, Bryan, 130, 149–152, 156–157, 160, 212
CEO, 218–221
cherries, 153–155
chess, 45–50, 56, 262
Chick-fil-A, 98–99, 189
China, 92, 261
Chodorov, Frank, 160, 162, 165
choice, 13, 54, 67, 74-75, 84, 87, 89, 115, 137, 151, 159–166, 172, 191, 236, 266
Coase, Ronald H., 6, 256
coffee, 11, 62, 87, 90, 134, 155, 193–194, 197, 253–256
college, 59, 79, 84, 106, 163, 200, 204, 208
competitive, 23, 66, 114, 147, 159, 179–180, 187, 233, 255, 258
consequences, 58–59, 88, 114, 170, 180, 186, 262–263, 267
consumers, 63, 99, 125, 131, 148, 154, 156, 188–190
consumption, 20, 133–135, 154, 188–189, 191
control, 50, 56, 92, 156, 169, 196, 214, 255, 263

cost, 12, 16, 21–22, 42, 56, 71, 74, 89, 99–100, 102-103, 105–107, 120–121, 125, 154–155, 157, 169, 171, 174–176, 180, 183, 187–189 195–196, 220, 233–234, 240, 250-251, 254–258, 267
cotton, 32, 205–209
countries, 13–14, 150, 240, 266
COVID, 14, 46–47, 77, 81, 169–171, 174–175, 183–185
Cowen, Tyler, 80, 109–110, 142, 217–223
cray, 194
cultural, 14, 17, 84, 161, 165, 208, 219
Currie-Knight, Kevin, 159-166

demand, 6, 22–23, 56, 66, 78, 89, 99, 147, 154, 174–175, 197, 220, 227, 230
democratic, 16, 123, 132, 213
division, 20, 50, 54–55, 62, 124, 134, 237
drugs, 87, 90, 185
drunk, 264
Duke, 235–237

economics, 4–8, 12, 16, 19–20, 22–23, 34, 37–38, 42–44, 46–47, 49–50, 53–54, 60, 65, 70, 84–85, 89, 109, 110, 120, 123–127, 131, 134-135, 139, 149–152, 154, 157, 170–171, 173, 179–181, 183–184, 189, 196, 205–209, 213, 220, 221, 230, 233-234, 242, 251, 255, 257, 261–267
economic growth, 11-17, 31, 34, 37–38, 43, 135, 190, 205–209, 219, 245
economy, 6, 34, 56, 65, 71, 111, 119, 124, 132–135, 153, 190–191, 206, 208–209, 211, 220, 242, 261
Edison, Thomas, 31, 33–34
education, 7, 78, 88, 159–168, 212, 244

effect, 99, 107, 120–121, 134, 150-151, 153–154, 180, 189-191, 195, 204, 207-208, 219
Ehrlich, Paul, 35–36
Elsa, 229-232
employ, 57–58, 142, 146, 251
employees, 87, 180, 250
energy, 12, 35, 61, 93, 167, 227, 250–251
engine, 221, 231
engineering, 62, 64, 78–79
Epstein, Gene, 172
essential, 22, 67, 124, 126, 207–208
ethics, 60, 92, 110, 134–135, 217, 262-263
exchange, 5, 20–22, 28, 54, 56–57, 60–61, 63, 71, 87, 89, 125–126, 132, 171, 240, 253
expand, 67, 78, 84, 189–192
exports, 35 206
externality, 183, 253–260

failure, 8, 123, 127, 183–184, 186
family, 26–27, 31, 44, 61, 78, 91–92, 107, 113, 120–121, 155, 230–231, 246
farmers, 28, 138, 153–155, 241
FDA, 184–186
financial, 12, 66–67, 80, 222, 233, 244, 264–265
financial return, 32, 66–67, 246
firms, 80, 106–107, 111, 134, 180–181, 189–191, 193–194, 196, 214, 218–220, 222–223, 251–252, 254, 265
food, 27, 78, 85, 91–93, 97–98, 114–115, 121, 138, 146, 167, 181
freedom, 84, 88, 150, 172, 199, 261
free market, 19, 27–29, 33–34, 72, 93, 99, 109-111, 159–160, 167, 173-174, 187, 194, 243-247,
Friedman, Milton, 159-166, 244

284

# Index

friends, 26–28, 33, 42, 61, 85, 93, 106–107, 113, 139, 147, 155, 157, 211, 213
Frozen, 229–232
future, 43, 88, 126, 130, 133, 174, 188, 227, 230, 242

game, 46–50, 60, 64, 145-147, 175, 196, 208, 219, 240, 263
global, 49, 129, 150–151, 185, 261
Goldberg, Jonah, 12, 15, 25
government, 45, 49, 53, 67, 93, 100, 110, 124, 141, 143, 151, 155, 159–164, 170–171, 184, 186, 219, 222, 243–246, 252, 255, 257–259, 262, 265
Gramm, Phil, 25–26
grow, 21–22, 62, 66-67, 154, 156, 206-207, 209, 253-254
guitar, 62
gun, 3

Haidt, Jonathan, 199-204
Hansen, Bradley A., 207
Harford, Tim, 1, 110, 187, 255
Hayek, F.A., 23, 25, 50, 54–56, 71, 107, 124-125, 127, 131-132, 134, 167, 169-170, 187-188, 191
Heyne, Paul T., 63, 256
Henderson, David, 170–171, 181
history, 12, 22, 42, 49, 54, 127, 142, 157, 165, 199, 205–206, 209, 230, 240–241, 243
Higgs, Robert, 171
Holcombe, Randall, 34, 88
Horwitz, Steven, 1, 139, 263
housing, 123, 167, 194–196
Huemer, Michael, 151

ideas, 3, 5, 8, 14, 17, 26, 49, 58–59, 75, 123, 130, 160, 162–163, 165, 169, 199–200, 204, 212, 222, 242, 266

immigration, 149–152
incentives, 8, 27, 49, 67, 75, 102, 111, 114, 125, 155, 157, 175, 184, 186, 240, 244, 251, 265
incomes, 12, 99, 141, 146–147, 153
industry, 57–58, 62, 100, 142, 155, 205, 245, 250
infinite, 32, 43, 47, 101
information, 6, 13, 47, 50, 56, 63, 78, 98, 105, 108, 110–111, 114, 126–127, 131, 169–170, 172, 187–189, 234
institutions, 16, 60, 110, 150, 161, 168, 170, 218–219, 241–242, 260
insurance, 28, 87, 246
interest, 33, 54, 57, 60–61, 71, 130, 134, 162, 169, 188–192, 194
invisible, 57, 61–64, 126, 167, 234, 256
iPhone, 27, 34, 120–121
iPod, 32–34

jobs, 33, 84, 88–89, 137–139, 150, 180, 185, 193, 231, 244, 250

Keynes, John Maynard, 132, 134, 221
Klein, Daniel, 165, 246
knowledge, 14, 20, 22–23, 25, 28, 56, 62–65, 78–79, 81, 89, 109–110, 126–127, 131–132, 143, 154, 161, 172, 174, 212, 227, 253

labor, 20–22, 54–55, 62, 87–89, 92, 97, 107, 120, 124, 134, 138, 146, 150–151, 154–155, 170–171, 179, 191, 193–194, 209, 211–214, 221, 237, 251, 264
land, 21, 62, 71, 125–126, 154, 191–192, 241, 257
Landsburg, Steven, 1, 8, 56, 99, 155, 195

left, 15, 72, 121, 161–162, 167–168, 201, 225–226, 244–245, 251
legislator, 169–170
leisure, 13, 88–89, 167–168, 221
Lewis, C.S., 26, 204
libertarian, 3, 19, 151, 160-164, 243, 253
lobbyists, 222, 251
losses, 99, 126–127, 131, 188, 250–251, 265
love, 7–8, 26–28, 88, 93, 107, 114, 218, 221, 232, 237, 242, 254, 266
Lukianoff, Greg, 199-204
luxury, 12, 195–196

magic, 19–21
Magness, Phillip, 160
Mandalorian, 239–242
Man of System, 45, 56, 58, 89, 212, 262
Margo, Robert, 206
Marx, Karl, Marxism, 132, 205, 222
market, 3, 6, 8, 19–20, 23, 27–29, 33–34, 42, 54-56, 60, 62–67, 72, 75, 88–90, 93, 97–99, 102, 107–111, 114–115, 124–127, 132, 138, 142, 146–148, 150-151, 154, 159–162, 167–168, 171–174, 179–180, 183, 187-189, 192, 194, 196, 213, 219-220, 225, 227, 233, 243–247, 255–256, 258, 260, 264-267, see also free market
Marketplace, 160, 165–166
material, 16–17, 38, 42, 55, 135
McCloskey, Deirdre N., 1, 11, 13, 16, 91, 217, 232, 243
means, 3, 14, 26, 32, 34, 38, 46–47, 56, 63, 74, 83–85, 92, 106, 109, 123–127, 131, 138, 162, 165, 172, 180, 183, 186, 188, 192, 195–196, 225–227, 229, 261, 267
Michigan, 153–156

Mind, 80, 167–170, 199, 204, 212–213
minds, 6, 34, 78, 81, 105, 168, 171
minimum, 58, 179–181, 193–194, 250, 264, 267
Mises, Ludwig von, 20, 55, 124–127, 131, 161
Mokyr, Joel, 16–17
monetary, 131, 188, 190
money, 6, 12, 32, 49, 57, 71, 78, 80, 87–88, 121, 124, 133, 135, 138–139, 141–143, 145, 153–155, 160, 176, 188, 190–191, 207, 222, 233, 237, 240, 250, 264–265, 267
moral, 16, 28, 59–61, 84, 111, 122, 135, 151–152, 157, 161, 164, 200, 262, 264
mortality, 14, 261, 266
Munger, Michael, 1, 71, 176, 233-234, 241
music, 14–15, 31–34, 37–39, 47, 134

national, 59, 120, 138, 145–146, 206, 267
natural, 12, 35, 55, 60, 69, 106, 120, 122
New York, 89, 179–181, 199
Nock, Albert J. 160–162, 165
noise, 39, 79, 254, 256–257
North, Douglass, 12, 43, 234, 241

Oaken, Wandering, 229–232
Octavius, Otto, 41–42
oil, 12, 17, 35, 154, 218, 226–227
online, 6, 46, 48–50, 78–80, 98, 175–176, 245
opportunities, 15, 33, 43, 97, 119, 123, 138, 169, 180, 219, 258
order, 6–7, 19–20, 28, 33, 50, 54, 56, 131, 148, 161, 170–172, 185, 187, 241, 244, 253, 258
organizations, 161, 214, 218–220, 246

# Index

Otteson, James, 167, 169, 212–213, 217, 227
outbreak, 106, 175
own, 21–22, 26, 32, 45–46, 55–57, 60–62, 70, 74, 107, 110, 125, 127, 131, 151, 161–162, 165, 169, 172, 185, 188, 195, 199, 201, 211, 213–214, 225, 230, 240, 244–245, 255, 262, 266
ownership, 92, 109, 125, 127, 131

pandemic, 14, 23, 46–47, 77, 79–81, 171, 183–184
pay, 32, 35, 67, 74, 87–88, 110, 129, 146, 151, 174–177, 180, 188–189, 219–221, 240, 244, 250, 255–257
pencil, 19–20, 78–79
person, 3, 13, 19, 26, 28, 34, 58–60, 75, 119, 124, 138, 143, 149, 157, 165, 170, 174–175, 185, 212, 227, 244, 256, 259, 262
police, 129, 243–246
policy, 7, 28, 85, 152, 157, 170, 184, 196–197, 200, 213, 260, 262-264, 267
political, 16, 65, 123, 150–151, 156–157, 168, 170, 219, 242, 244, 265, 267
pollution, 255
population, 13–14, 92, 222, 227, 259
private, 3, 20, 32, 54, 58, 92, 109, 125–126, 131–132, 135, 142, 155, 160–162, 171, 176, 183, 239–240, 244–246, 259, 265
privileges, 54, 100, 251
production, productivity, 13, 20–21, 32, 34, 38, 56, 62–63, 67, 89, 92, 106, 109, 111, 115, 120, 124–127, 130–132, 134, 147, 150-151, 154–155, 165, 167, 170, 175, 184, 188–190, 192, 194, 207, 209, 218, 229–232, 245,
profit, 57, 62-63, 67, 92, 114, 126, 131, 174, 176, 188, 191, 194, 226–227, 251, 264-265
progress, 15–17, 34, 37–38, 42, 44, 46–47, 55, 206, 261
protection, 17, 130, 200, 243–246

Rand, Ayn, 8, 160, 164, 166
rate, 13–14, 16, 49, 79, 100, 134, 188–192
rational, 54, 125, 131, 134, 156–157, 203, 265
regulation, 92, 98–101, 110, 114, 156, 181, 184, 196, 245, 255, 258, 260
resources, 17, 35-36 62–63, 67, 100, 109, 121–122, 125–127, 131, 138–139, 142, 154–155, 161, 188–190, 203, 220, 222, 227, 240–241, 244, 250–252, 255–256, 265, 267
restaurant, 15, 85, 98-99 106–107, 110, 115, 121, 181, 188-192, 196, 213, 254,
retiree, 256–257
revenue, 57, 61, 102, 147
Ricardo, David, 21–23
Richter, Eugen, 130
Ridley, Matt, 34
rights, 3, 16, 20, 60, 147, 152, 203, 256–257
roads, 141, 151, 243, 246–247
Rose, David C., 111
Rosling, Hans, 11, 13–14
Rothbard, Murray, 160, 164
rulers, 16-17, 184
rules, 47, 50, 56, 85, 97, 100, 138, 184, 194, 213, 240, 245, 251, 258–259

safety, 101–103, 130, 194, 200–202
Samuel Adams Brewery, 65–66

287

Sanders, Bernie, 123, 211–214
saving, 55, 99, 134–135, 154, 188–191
school, 65, 78, 88, 98–99 110, 126, 134, 141, 159–165, 204, 213, 255
Schumpeter, Joseph A., 31
Scott, James C., 168
self-checkout, 137-139
Shakespeare, 42
Simon, Julian, 34–36, 70
Simpsons, 259
slavery, 205–209, 266
Smith, 20, 26, 43, 45, 53–56, 59–62, 72, 100, 106, 110, 142, 164, 167, 197, 212, 226–227, 262
Smith, Adam, 20, 26, 45, 53-64, 72, 106, 142, 164, 167, 197, 212, 226-227, 262,
Smith, Vernon, 43, 110, 227
soccer, 147–148
social, 5–7, 20, 26, 46, 48, 54, 56, 58–59, 79–80, 85, 105–106, 114, 124, 127, 139, 149, 157, 162, 164–165, 167–168, 170–171, 173–174, 183, 213, 219, 221–222, 230, 232, 242, 244, 250–251, 255, 263
socialism, 19, 55, 59, 123–127, 129–132, 173, 212–214, 255, see also magic
society, 5, 43, 45–46, 50, 55–57, 61, 81, 89, 105, 111, 125, 131–132, 160, 169, 212, 227, 232, 260, 262–263
Solo, Han, 208–209
Sowell, Thomas, 1, 43, 53, 80, 120, 124, 149, 163
specialization, 22, 61–62, 132, 236–237
spending, 100, 133–134, 148, 154–155, 159, 191, 196, 222, 229, 240
Spider-Man, 41–44, 209
spillover, 159, 243, 254, 257–258
Star-Wars, 43, 208-209, 239-242

state, 12, 64, 66, 77, 98, 100, 106, 124, 141, 151, 161–162, 165, 167–170, 174, 176, 212, 243, 245–246
statesman, 58, 142
stranger, 25–26, 31, 34, 75, 85, 107, 113–115, 213,
Stringham, Edward, 240, 244
Sun-Tzu, 46
supply, 6, 22–23, 87–89, 93, 119, 155, 174, 189, 195–197, 220, 225, 227, 230, 252, 258

Taco-Bell, 196
Target, 63, 71, 231
tariffs, 7, 153–157, 251–252
taxation, 119, 122, 141-142, 151, 217, 256–258, 267
theft, 249–252, see also taxation
time, 7–8, 12–13, 15, 20–21, 23, 25, 33–35, 46–49, 55, 59, 61–63, 65, 70–71, 75, 80, 88–89, 93, 100, 102, 106–107, 110, 114, 120, 124, 126-127, 130, 133, 138, 143, 145, 147, 149, 152–153, 156, 160–162, 164, 168, 174–177, 181, 189–191, 208, 221, 227, 231, 240, 245, 247, 249–251, 259, 263, 265, 267
toilet, 174–176
Tucker, Jeffrey, 2, 93

Uber, 50, 74–75, 114

wage, 23, 58, 84, 87–90, 100, 138, 148, 150, 179–181, 191, 193-194 250, 264, 267
Walmart, 7, 71, 85, 134
war, 59, 126, 239–240
Weinersmith, Zach, 149-150
welfare, 20, 92, 125, 151, 243, 245–246
Williamson, Zion, 235–237

## Index

work, 16, 19–20, 27, 46, 55, 60, 63, 73, 75, 77, 79–80, 83–84, 87–88, 90, 99–100, 106–107, 119–120, 123–124, 131, 134–135, 146, 148, 167, 184, 188, 207, 218, 220–221, 240–241, 245, 249, 256
workers, 129, 137, 146–148, 173, 180–181, 214, 219–220

World Cup, 145–148
world class, 148–149, 236
Wright, Gavin, 206–209
Wright, Robert E., 209

Yelp, 98, 106–107, 114
YouTube, 39, 48, 80, 134

# ABOUT THE
# LIBERTARIAN CHRISTIAN INSTITUTE

The Libertarian Christian Institute is a federal 501(c)(3) tax-exempt educational and religious nonprofit organization that promotes libertarianism from a Christian point of view. We are convinced that libertarianism is the most consistent expression of Christian political thought. LCI is ecumenical in nature, welcoming all those who confess the traditional creeds of the universal church.

Our goals are to persuade our fellow Christians through online programs, physical publications, in-person conferences, and regional small group meetups, and to love our fellow libertarians as Jesus would have us do. Our online presence is unmatched in the libertarian community, with hundreds of articles, book reviews, videos, podcasts, news reports, and much more. Dr. Horn is regularly sought after for a Christian libertarian perspective on a variety of political and cultural topics. Most recently, our Christians For Liberty Conferences have brought hundreds of Christian Libertarians together to share and to learn from great speakers in Austin, Texas. As the organization grows, we are actively seeking out donors who desire to see an organization such as this make a positive difference in the church and in the world today for liberty and for Christ.

As the Libertarian Christian Institute grows, we are actively seeking out donors who desire to see an organization such as this make a positive difference in the church and in the world today for liberty and for Christ. If you would like to participate in our mission to equip the church to make the Christian case for a free society, join us by visiting libertarianchristians.com/donate.

## Our Vision: Christians Embracing a Free Society

The Libertarian Christian Institute envisions a world where Christians around the world promote the values and principles of a free society as the most consistent expression of Christian political thought. We see a world where, instead of polarizing to the left or right, Christians demonstrate that individual liberty is a force for the common good. We aim to persuade Christians that the political expression of our faith inclines us toward the principles of individual liberty and free markets.

## Our Mission: Equipping Christians to Spread the Message of Individual Liberty

We seek to create quality resources to equip Christians to promote individual liberty among their families, friends, ministries, and churches. We view ourselves as a contributor to the vast resources of libertarian content online by making the Christian case for a free society. We resist the assumption that the default political position of Christianity is domination and control, and we combat this by employing studies in history, theology, and biblical exegesis in a variety of venues.

# THE LIBERTARIAN CHRISTIAN INSTITUTE'S CORE VALUES

We believe that every Christian libertarian should feel comfortable affirming our Core Values, even if they have their own nuance or "spin" on them. Our aim is not to comprehensively spell out what every Christian libertarian must believe, but provide a central set of tenets that we can all start from, regardless of differences in denomination or theological inclinations.

## 1. Christian Political Philosophy Should be Informed by a Holistic View of Scripture, Reason, and Historical Theology

A comprehensive view of the biblical narrative indicates that the Church's proclamation of Jesus' lordship is not a mere personal statement of allegiance; it is also an anti-imperial declaration that the way of peace comes through Christ's counter-cultural kingdom of love and service. Followers of Christ are called to be a prophetic voice against the powers of domination and violence. The State — the monopolized institution of force in society — is never to be confused with the Kingdom of God, and when the power of the state grows, the rightful influence of churches, families, and local communities is diminished.

## 2. A Free And Civil Society Depends Upon Respect For The Non-Aggression Principle

The ethics modeled by Christ and the early Church call us to change the world and build the Kingdom of God through service rather than force; through persuasion rather than coercion. The use of political force to compel ethical behavior cannot change hearts and only antagonizes our struggle against sin, death, and evil. Christians must call for repentance from sin in humility and never with violence. As such, a consistently Christian ethic always embodies non-aggression.

## 3. Individual Liberty and the Common Good are not at Odds

As God is intrinsically relational within the Trinity, so also human beings are created to live in community. Sin has marred the communal relationships for which we were created by pitting individuals against God, against one another, and against the earth for which we are called to be wise stewards. Affirming the dignity, worth, and rights of the individual as an image-bearer of God is a first step toward restoring authentic, Christ-centered community among diverse individuals. Because society is comprised of individuals, a healthy society requires healthy individuals. Through voluntary cooperation and respect for freedom, people can join together to trade, innovate, create, collaborate, share, and build a world that simultaneously respects the individual and betters our neighbor.

## 4. Social Institutions Matter for Human Flourishing

Humans are created to be social beings, and God's design is that we work together to develop institutions which promote human flourishing. Insofar as these institutions are voluntary, peaceful, and non-coercive, human beings possess the God-given capacity to solve the worst of problems in the best of ways. Social institutions founded upon mutual cooperation — such as marriage, family, church, organizations, and businesses — are vital for authentic humanity.

## 5. Christian Theology Affirms the Essential Tenets of Free Market Economics

Respect for private property, voluntary exchange, condemnation of theft, and the value of cooperation and service towards achieving common goals flow naturally from Christian thought and habit. This is what defines "capitalism" in the libertarian view. Wealth is a tool given by God, and all who possess such wealth are expected to utilize it for God's Kingdom and the good of our neighbor. Taxation and regulation tend to destroy wealth, discourage innovation, and centralize power, and therefore hamper our ability to fulfill the calling of God. Where free markets are allowed to flourish, human beings will prosper both materially and spiritually. Additionally, Christian ethics helps equip our economies for service toward God and neighbor.

Even if you don't call yourself a libertarian, if you share our affinity for these core values, we count you among our ranks. We hope that you will want to partner with us to help spread the message of liberty by making the Christian case for a free society. Help us keep the message alive and growing at libertarianchristians.com

**GIVE TO LCI TODAY!**

# FAITH SEEKING FREEDOM
## Libertarian Christian Answers to Tough Questions

Discussing Christian faith and politics is tough. If you're tired of the typical left/right answers that sound like they were pulled from last night's cable news, then you need a new way of thinking about faith and politics. This book will help you take your political conversations to the next level.

In Faith Seeking Freedom, the Libertarian Christian Institute has gathered together some of the brightest minds at the intersection of Christianity and libertarianism to collect brief but thoughtful answers to over a hundred questions frequently posed to liberty-loving believers.

In this book, you will find answers to questions like:

Should Christians care about politics?

- What does God have to say about government?
- What makes somebody a libertarian?
- Why are property rights so important?
- And many more!

Available in the following formats:

- Softcover
- Kindle
- Audiobook

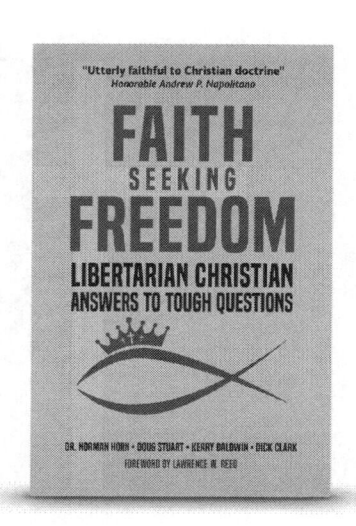

Find more at **FaithSeekingFreedom.com**

# LOVE PODCASTS?

## Check out the Christians for Liberty Network!

The Christians for Liberty Network is a collection of podcasts, shows, and other media featuring the voices and perspectives of a diverse group of libertarian Christians.

Whether you're looking for an exegetical take on Romans 13, the libertarian Christian angle on the news, how the Bible displays the prophetic voice against empire, or if you simply have a question that needs a solid answer, the Christians for Liberty Network will be your favorite source!

Visit **Christiansforliberty.net** to listen!

Made in the USA
Middletown, DE
05 May 2024